BURT FRANKLIN: RESEARCH & SOURCE WORKS SERIES 561
American Classics in History & Social Science 149

THE FORMATION OF THE REPUB-LICAN PARTY AS A NATIONAL POLITICAL ORGANIZATION

THE REPUBLICAN PLATFORM

CONTAINING

THE LIVES OF

FREMONT AND DAYTON,

WITH BEAUTIFUL STEEL PORTRAITS OF EACH,
AND THEIR LETTERS OF ACCEPTANCE.

ALSO,

THE DECLARATION OF INDEPENDENCE,

AND THE

CONSTITUTION OF THE UNITED STATES.

BOSTON:
PUBLISHED BY JOHN P. JEWETT AND COMPANY.
CLEVELAND, OHIO:
JEWETT, PROCTOR AND WORTHINGTON.
NEW YORK: SHELDON, BLAKEMAN AND COMPANY
1856.

Photographic reprint of the title page of the first Republican national campaign text book ever issued.

(See footnote 2, page 48.)

THE FORMATION OF THE REPUB-
LICAN PARTY AS A NATIONAL
POLITICAL ORGANIZATION

BY

GORDON S. P. KLEEBERG, A.M., LL.M.

BURT FRANKLIN
NEW YORK

Published by LENOX HILL Pub. & Dist. Co. (Burt Franklin)
235 East 44th St., New York, N.Y. 10017
Originally Published: 1911
Reprinted: 1970
Printed in the U.S.A.

S.B.N. 8337-1936X
Library of Congress Card Catalog No.: 71-132681
Burt Franklin: Research and Source Works Series 561
American Classics in History and Social Science 149

To My Father

CONTENTS

CHAPTER I

CHAPTER II

CHAPTER III

CHAPTER IV

CHAPTER I

INTRODUCTORY

The period from 1851 to 1859 is an age of transition in which old political alignments in the United States were broken and gave place to new crystallizations of voters; and in which also former political issues were supplanted by the paramount contest over slavery in the Territories.

The passage of the Kansas-Nebraska Bill [1] in 1854 sounded the death knell of the Whig party. The section of the bill which expressly repealed the Missouri Compromise demonstrated to opponents of slavery everywhere [2] that the Western Territory could be re-

[1] The Missouri Compromise, it was supposed, forever prohibited slavery in the Territory of Nebraska (the northern portion of the Louisiana Purchase). Stephen A. Douglas, chairman of the committee on Territories in the Senate introduced this bill in 1854, wherein it was proposed to leave to the inhabitants of Nebraska the decision as to whether or not they would have slavery. His bill declared that the slavery restriction of the Missouri Compromise, because "inconsistent with the principles of the legislation of 1850 (commonly called the Compromise Measures) was superseded by it," and was "hereby declared inoperative and void," and divided the great Territory of Nebraska into two parts, calling the northern portion Nebraska and the southern Kansas. Hereafter each Territory whether north or south of the parallel of 36° 30' should be perfectly free to admit or exclude slavery as its people should decide. This made a clear division between Northern and Southern Whigs as was evidenced by the vote in the Senate on March 4th when the bill passed, every Northern Whig voting against it and nine Southern Whigs voting for it.

[2] New York *Herald,* October 13th and November 10th, 1854.

served for free labor only by a powerful political party, definitely committed to the exclusion of that peculiar institution from this domain.

On May 9th, 1854, the day after the passage of the Bill by the House of Representatives, some thirty members of Congress, at the invitation of Israel Washburn of Maine, came together at the rooms of Thomas G. Elliott and Edward Dickinson of Massachusetts, and agreed to form a new party to be called the Republican party.[1] While those events were occurring in Congress, frequent non-partisan meetings were being held in many of the Northern States looking toward the formation of a new party, now that the old stereotyped party organizations were being rent asunder on the Kansas-Nebraska issue. This course was also warmly and persistently urged by many newspapers, especially by the New York *Tribune*.

It was not long before the opponents of slavery extension in the Territories began to draw together and assume the form of political organizations. One of the earliest, if not the earliest, of the movements that contemplated definite action toward the formation of a new party, took place in Ripon, Wisconsin, on February 28th, 1854.[2] After a thorough canvass, conference and general comparison of views, initiated by Mr. Alvan E. Bovay, a prominent member of the Whig party, among the Whigs, Free Soilers and Democrats of that township, a call was issued signed by himself representing

[1] H. Wilson, *Rise and Fall of the Slave Power,* II, 411; F. Curtis, *The Republican Party,* I, 179.

[2] H. Wilson, *Rise and Fall of the Slave Power,* II, 410, 412; G. M. Harvey, *The Chautauquan,* September, 1897, vol. XVI, N. S., p. 643.

the Whigs, and by a representative of each of the other two parties, for a Republican meeting to consider the grave issues which were assuming an aspect of such alarming importance. The meeting was largely attended by persons of both sexes from the town and surrounding country and a resolution was adopted that, if the Nebraska Bill then pending in the Senate should pass, they would "throw old party organizations to the wind and organize a new party on the sole issue of non-extension of slavery." At a second meeting [1] held on the 20th of March, 1854, the day after the passage of the bill, in the same place, by formal vote of the assembly, the town committees of the Whig and Free Soil parties were dissolved and a committee of five, consisting of three Whigs, one Free Soiler and a Democrat was chosen to begin the work of forming a new party.

Similar local organizations sprang up rapidly in other Northern States very soon after this radical departure made in Wisconsin. For example, in Illinois, local attempts made early in 1854 to disband the Whig party and form a new party were quite successful. In Maine, on August 7th, 1854, a meeting, in the nature of a delegate county convention,[2] and one of the first regularly organized delegate conventions [3] which as-

[1] Rhodes, *History of the United States*, II, 47, 48; F. Curtis, *The Republican Party*, I, 174; Julian, *Political Recollections*, 144; New York *Tribune*, June 24, 1854.

[2] W. F. P. Fogg, *History of the Formation of the Republican Party in Maine*.

[3] Correspondence of Joseph H. Manley with Francis Curtis; see F. Curtis, *The Republican Party*, I, 193, 194, 208, 211, also New York *Tribune*, August 20th, 1884. See also footnote to p. 22, *infra*.

sumed the name of Republican in a formal manner, was held at Strong and the Republican party was launched in that State.[1]

Out of this disintegration of local organizations and reconstruction of local machinery proceeded at length new Republican State-wide organizations.[2]

The first Republican State mass convention [3] which adopted a platform and nominated a full State ticket was held at Jackson, Michigan, on July 6th, 1854.[4] The example thus set was speedily followed in some

[1] F. Curtis, *The Republican Party,* I, 193.

[2] Address of Wm. Barnes, Sr., of Nantucket, Massachusetts, the son-in-law of Thurlow Weed, delivered at the Golden Jubilee of the Republican party, Philadelphia, June 17th, 1906 (Published by A. B. Burke, Philadelphia, 1906). See footnote to page 38, *infra.*

Hon. William Barnes, Sr., a lawyer of Nantucket, Massachusetts, and the son-in-law of Thurlow Weed was actively identified with the convention which nominated Fremont and the later one which nominated Lincoln. His son, William Barnes, Jr., is the editor of the *Evening Journal* at Albany and at present the State chairman of the Republican party in New York. The writer was informed by Governor Stewart L. Woodford, that Mr. Barnes, Sr., kept a diary during all the early years of the Republican party and that he was probably the most accurately informed of any of the early living Republicans. The writer has had the privilege of corresponding with Mr. Barnes and had hoped to have, prior to the publication of this work, the advantage of reading some of his reminiscences concerning the early Republican party movements with which Mr. Barnes was so actively connected and which he was advised were in course of publication, but the necessity of completing this work within the prescribed time limit has prevented this.

[3] A complete record of the convention may be found in the Detroit *Free Democrat,* and the Jackson *Citizen,* July 7th, 1854. (Cited in Curtis, I, 181 *et seq.*)

[4] *Life of Zachariah Chandler,* published by the Detroit *Post and Tribune,* 1880, page 109 *et seq.* F. Curtis, *The Republican Party,* I, 180, *et seq.* Hon. John Hay, Secretary of State of the United States delivered a famous address here July 6th, 1904, the fiftieth anniversary of the birth of the Republican party in that State.

form in other States. At Montpelier, Vermont, on July 13th, 1854,[1] a convention was held which selected a delegation to a national convention (in case one should be called), consisting of one Free Soiler, three Whigs and one anti-slavery Democrat. Also at Madison, Wisconsin, on the 13th of July, 1854,[2] a convention was held, at which a "Republican" State executive committee was chosen and the organization of the new party in that State further perfected. Republican conventions were likewise held at Columbus, Ohio,[3] and in the State of Indiana [4] on the same day [5] as in Vermont and Wisconsin. The convention at Columbus was in the nature of an anti-Nebraska mass convention. A State organization was formed similar to that at the Jackson convention,[6] and while the name Republican was not adopted until the following year, the movement resulted in sending a solid anti-Nebraska convention to Congress by a large majority.[7] In Indiana also the name Republican was not formally employed until the following year but an anti-slavery platform was put forth and a ticket nominated.[8]

---

[1] F. Curtis, *The Republican Party*, I, 193.

[2] *Life of Chandler, supra*, 113.

[3] Shucker, *Life of Chase*, 165.

[4] G. W. Julian, *Political Recollections*, 144; T. C. Smith, *Liberty and Free Soil Parties in the Northwest*, page 290.

[5] The day was chosen because it was the anniversary of the enactment of the Ordinance of 1787 and for the same reason was selected by Wisconsin, Vermont and Indiana (Rhodes, *History of the United States*, II, 49).

[6] T. C. Smith, *Liberty & Free Soil Parties in the Northwest*, 295.

[7] Rhodes, *History of the United States*, II, 60.

[8] T. C. Smith, *Liberty & Free Soil Parties, etc.*, page 290, *et seq.*

One of the earliest local mass meetings, at which the name "Republican"[1] was adopted, was that held at Friendship, Alleghany County, New York, on May 16th, 1854,[2] called through the efforts of A. N. Cole, the editor of the Genesee Valley *Free Press*. At this meeting a committee was appointed to call a nominating convention, which subsequently met pursuant to this call at Angelica, New York, October 18th, 1854, and nominated county officers. This was followed by county mass meetings, under the name of "Republican" at Albany, July 28th, 1854, and New York City, August 8th, 1854,[3] at both of which delegates were elected to a State convention to be held at Saratoga Springs, August 16th, 1854. The example set by Albany and New York, was followed by all the other counties in the State except three.[4]

The convention, composed of the delegates aggregating between 400 and 500,[5] appointed at the several county mass meetings, met at Saratoga on the 16th of August, 1854,[6] and was the first regular delegate State

[1] Address of Wm. Barnes, Sr., etc., page 71.

[2] Curtis, *The Republican Party*, I, 202, *et seq.;* Address of Wm. Barnes, Sr., etc., see footnote to page 16, *supra;* Rhodes, *History of the United States*, II, 65.

[3] New York *Tribune,* August 8th, 1854.

[4] Suffolk, Schoharie and Schenectady.

[5] *Proceedings of the Saratoga Springs Semi-Centennial, held September 14, 1904* (two pamphlets printed and published by Wm. Barnes, Sr.).

[6] *Ibid.*

Five delegates were sent from each Assembly district in the State. These delegates were appointed by mass meetings in each county, some attended by more than 1,000 voters.

convention of the Republican party held in New York,[1] though the convention itself took no definite action toward the formation of a new party, save endorsing[2] the policies of those States[3] which had already taken steps in that direction. It then adjourned to meet on September 26th, at Auburn. At this adjourned meeting a proposition to form a new party was introduced and debated but failed of adoption. A State ticket however was nominated and a State committee appointed.

In the following year the New York Whigs under the leadership of William H. Seward joined the Republican ranks, thus greatly adding to the strength of the New York Republican State organization.

On September 26th, 1855, the Republican and Whig State committees having called respective State conventions to meet on that day at Syracuse, the Whigs, who had met in a separate hall, marched in a body into the Republican State convention, participated in it, and helped to adopt a strong anti-slavery platform and to

[1] Springfield *Republican* (cited by Curtis, I, 205), August 17, 1854.

See also *Semi-centennial of the Republican Party, Proceedings at the Celebration at Saratoga Springs, September 14, 1905,* by William Barnes, Sr., one of the delegates from Albany County to the Saratoga Convention, August 16, 1854.

Mr. Wm. Barnes, Sr. regards this as the first regular delegate state convention of the Republican party ever held and maintains that the Jackson convention mentioned above was called as a mass convention and not as a regular delegate convention. He therefore claims that the foundation of the party was not laid at Jackson, Michigan as many contend but in the State of New York.

[2] Springfield *Republican,* August 18, 1854. (Cited by Curtis, I, 205.)

[3] Connecticut, Vermont, Iowa, Ohio, Indiana and Michigan.

nominate a State ticket under the name "Republican."[1]

In Massachusetts, a State mass convention was held at Worcester, July 20th, 1854,[2] and over 2500 persons responded to the call, which had been issued by a large number of the leading public men of the State.[3] A set of resolutions or platform was adopted and a call issued for a Republican State nominating convention, which met at Worcester, September 7th[4] of that year, nominated a State ticket under the name "Republican," and adopted a platform.[5] The Republican State organization was further perfected in the State of Massachusetts in the following year by a State convention held at Worcester on September 20th, 1855,[6] at which Nathaniel P. Banks, later to become the first Republican Speaker of the House of Representatives, presided. It formally adopted the name "Republican," appointed a large and able State central committee, nominated a full State ticket and promulgated an elaborate platform.

Several States which had failed to organize a Republican party in 1854, did so in 1855. It was in that

---

[1] New York *Tribune*, September 27, 1855.

[2] Springfield *Daily Republican*, July 21st, 1854.   (Cited by Curtis, I, 195.)

[3] *Ibid*, July 10, 1854.   *Ibid*.

[4] *Ibid*, September 8th, 1854.   *Ibid*.

[5] The full text of the resolutions is published in the Springfield *Daily Republican* of September 8, 1854, and in Curtis, *The Republican Party*, I, 200.

[6] A full account of the proceedings of the convention together with the platform is to be found in the Springfield *Daily Republican*, September 21, 1855.   (Cited by Curtis I, 200.)

year that Ohio came into line, by completing a Republican organization.[1] A delegate State convention was called in that State and a State ticket under the name "Republican" nominated, and subsequently elected.[2]

The first State convention of the Republican party in Pennsylvania was held at Pittsburg on the 5th of September, 1855,[3] at which a full State ticket was nominated and a platform adopted, under the name of "Republican."

Later, but none the less effectively, Illinois perfected her Republican State organization, by holding a Republican State convention at Bloomington on May 29th, 1856, at the call of some fifteen Illinois editors of anti-Nebraska newspapers. At this convention, a platform was adopted, a Republican State ticket nominated and delegates appointed to the national Republican convention[4] to be held at Philadelphia in the following month.

Connecticut was one of the last Northern States to form a regular distinct Republican State organization.[5] Although a Republican convention had been held at Hartford in that State in the spring of 1856, to nominate candidates for State offices, it was a mass. meeting rather than a delegate convention and it was not until 1858 that a regular Republican convention

---

[1] New York *Tribune*, June 28, 1855.

[2] Pike, *First Blows of the Civil War*, 299.

[3] A. K. McClure, *Our Presidents and How We Make Them*, 136.

[4] See *infra*, page 38.

[5] F. Curtis, *The Republican Party*, I, 226, 228.

was called, by means of a State committee, and the party may be regarded as organized in that State.

Thus at the opening of the presidential year, 1856, Republican groups, having come into being during the two preceding years almost simultaneously [1] in different parts of the West, in New England and in the Middle States, the party, through the formation of committees and the holding of mass and delegate, State and local conventions, had reached a high degree of organization (as far as local units were concerned) and had developed, in many States, State-wide machinery for the promulgation of its political principles and purposes. This was now ready to be built into an imposing national machine in accordance with the approved traditions of the older political parties.

---

[1] "The place and the time where the Republican party was first organized will, I presume, remain like the birthplace of Homer, a subject of unending dispute. Seven cities claimed the latter and seven States may claim the former." (Address of James G. Blaine, delivered at Strong, Maine, August 19, 1884, published in the New York *Tribune,* August 20, 1884.)

CHAPTER II

THE REPUBLICAN NATIONAL CONVENTIONS
OF 1856 AND 1860

The Republican party having been formed in the various Northern States, the next step was to establish unity among these new local organizations and prepare for the presidential campaign of 1856. Its first influence of a national character was seen in the Thirty-fourth Congress when, on the hundred and thirty-third ballot, Nathaniel P. Banks was elected as the first Republican speaker of the House of Representatives.

In a sense, of course, the birth of the Republican party can be traced to the movements described in the preceding chapter. In fact, many ascribe its origin to the Free-Soil party which appeared in 1848, but, as a formal national machine, the Republican party was not ready for concerted work until 1856, when its first national convention met at Philadelphia and the organization of the party for the nation at large took place.

The germ [1] of this national organization was formed

---

[1] Mr. Clephane has compiled an interesting pamphlet on the birth of the Republican party in which the claim is very broadly made that the initiatory proceedings toward the organization of the Republican party were commenced by the Republican Association of Washington in 1855, and lead up to the February convention in Pittsburg in 1856. It is the old case of the many cities claiming "Homer dead," but it certainly was the germ of the national organization.

in the City of Washington on the 19th of June, 1855. On that date, "The Republican Association of Washington, District of Columbia" was created,—in reality, little more than a small club of which Lewis Clephane was the secretary—and it issued a "Declaration, Platform and Constitution," the preamble of which was as follows:

Whereas, by the repeal of the eighth section of the act for the admission of Missouri into the Union, the Territories of Kansas and Nebraska have been opened to the introduction of slavery and all the compromises real or imaginary upon that subject are thus violated and annulled and deep dishonor inflicted upon the age in which we live.

Now, therefore, in co-operation with all those throughout the land who oppose this and other similar measures which we deem to be contrary to the spirit of the Constitution and which are designed to extend and perpetuate slavery, we do associate ourselves together under the name and title of The Republican Association of Washington, District of Columbia.

The platform [1] embodied the principle "that Congress possessed no power over the institution of slavery in the several States but that outside of State jurisdiction, the constitutional powers of the Federal government should be exerted to secure life, liberty and happiness to all men," and that, "therefore there should be neither slavery nor involuntary servitude, except for the punishment of crime, in any of the Territories of the United States."

No president was elected at the first meeting of the

---

[1] The full text of the platform is printed in F. Curtis, *The Republican Party,* I, 249.

Association, and although efforts were made to induce Francis P. Blair, Sr., to accept the office, he declined.

Little more was heard of the Association until January 17th, 1856, when it issued a circular to the friends of the Republican movement throughout the United States appealing to the country to organize similar clubs. It was entitled "A Circular to the Friends of the Republican Movement throughout the United States."

The paper was signed by Daniel R. Goodloe, H. S. Brown and Lewis Clephane and stated that the signers had been appointed a committee on behalf of the Association to issue this circular letter to all Republican friends urging upon their attention the importance of organizing clubs or associations in every city and town to carry on a political campaign. The purpose of the Association was stated to be "to act in concert with the Republican members of Congress and all associations that may be formed throughout the States similar to our own as a 'National Committee' [1] for the dissemination of political information among the masses." The circular likewise stated, "We have taken a hall in a central position, established a reading room for the benefit of our visiting Republican friends and have made arrangements for the issue in phamphlet form of all important speeches that may be made during the present Congress" and closed with a request for the prompt formation of a local association and the open-

---

[1] This, although often referred to as the earliest Republican national committee was not a national committee in the sense in which the term is employed to-day in political literature. See *infra,* chapter IV.

ing of correspondence with the Washington Association.

The Association published and distributed among the people a number of pamphlets favoring the principles of the Republican party.[1]   Much of the labor attending its operation was performed by members of the Association without any pecuniary consideration as it had no other fund at its disposal than what it realized from the sale of its publications and the voluntary contributions of its members and friends.

About the same time the Pittsburg *Gazette,* the most pronounced anti-slavery Whig paper in Pennsylvania, became extremely active in the Republican cause.   Its editor Mr. D. N. White and his assistant Mr. Russell Errett toward the close of the year 1855, were consulted by David Wilmot of Pennsylvania and Lawrence Brainerd of Vermont (chairmen of the Republican State committees of their respective States) and a definite line of action was agreed upon.[2]   Up to this time, with the exception of the Washington Association's efforts, no definite attempt had been made anywhere or by any person to weld the various local organizations, which had sprung up, into a national party.

---

[1] *"Republican Campaign Documents of 1856.* A collection of the most important speeches and documents issued by the Republican Association of Washington, D. C., during the Presidential campaign of 1856." Published by Lewis Clephane, Secretary of the Republican Association, Washington, D. C., 1857; also a preface by Lewis Clephane.

[2] Address of Mr. William Barnes, Sr., of Nantucket, Massachusetts, delivered at the Golden Jubilee Celebration of the Republican party June 17th, 1906, at Philadelphia. (Published by A. B. Burk, Philadelphia, 1906.)

As a result of their conferences a call for a convention signed by two of these men, Brainerd and Wilmot, was issued from Washington, D. C., on January 17th, 1856, the same day on which the Washington Association issued its "circular."

When first issued it was signed by the chairmen of the Republican State committees of five [1] States and read as follows:

To the Republicans of the United States:

In accordance with what appears to be the general desire of the Republican Party, and at the suggestion of a large portion of the Republican press, the undersigned, chairmen of the State Republican Committees[2] of Maine, Vermont, Massachusetts, New York, Pennsylvania, Ohio, Michigan, Indiana and Wisconsin, hereby invite the Republicans of the Union to meet in informal convention at Pittsburg, on the 22nd of February, 1856, for the purpose of perfecting the National organization and providing for a National Delegate Convention of the Republican Party at some subsequent day to nominate candidates for the Presidency and Vice-Presidency to be supported at the election in November, 1856.

> A. P. STONE, of Ohio.
> J. Z. GOODRICH, of Mass.
> DAVID WILMOT, of Pa.
> LAWRENCE BRAINERD, of Vt.
> WILLIAM A. WHITE, of Wis.

Except for the fact that Wilmot, Brainerd, White and Errett were instrumental in the issuance of the call, little else seems to be known of its exact origin.

---

[1] Other signatures were subsequently added.

[2] This self-appointed body did not style itself a national committee though to some extent it might have done so. See *infra,* Chapter IV.

Apparently no record of the meeting of these chairmen is in existence and it seems doubtful whether
they ever formally met. The inference would be that
it was arranged by correspondence and by casual meetings between the various signers at Washington. The
late Mr. Cephas Brainerd,[1] who favored the writer with
an interview, was of the opinion that these gentlemen,
who were all Senators or Congressmen, knew one another from having met at various times in Washington
or at political gatherings elsewhere and that the call
was probably arranged by correspondence and sent
from one to the other to be signed. This would account for the fact, noted above, that when first issued
it only bore the five signatures shown above and that
others were subsequently appended. This view is
shared by General Stewart L. Woodford,[2] with whom
the writer was also fortunate in obtaining an interview.

The Republican Association of Washington doubtless had some share also in the issuance of the call of
January 17th, 1856, and probably took an active part
in the preliminary arrangements.[3]

In 1856, pursuant to separate preliminary correspondence, and to the above call from the Republican

[1] Mr. Brainerd was a distant relative of the signer of the call of
the similar name and was himself active in Republican politics a
year or so later, serving on the committee which arranged for
Lincoln's famous Cooper Institute speech in New York, February
27, 1860.

[2] General Woodford was secretary of the Republican central committee of the State of New York (the predecessor of the present
county committee) in 1857.

[3] Leslie's *History of the Republican Party,* I, Chapters I and II.
G. O. Seilhaimer (1900).

State chairmen of Maine, Vermont, Massachusetts, New York, Pennsylvania, Ohio, Michigan, Indiana and Wisconsin, a general meeting of prominent Republicans and anti-Nebraska politicians from all parts of the North and even from a few slave States took place at Pittsburg on February 22nd.[1] On the evening of February 21st an informal meeting of delegates to the convention was held in the parlors of the Monongahela Hotel, Pittsburg, for the purpose of making the preliminary arrangements for the convention. After consultation it was decided to have the several delegations select one man from each State and request these men to meet at eight o'clock next morning. At that meeting a plan for the organization of the convention, including the selection of Hon. Francis P. Blair, Sr., for president of the convention was adopted, and the Reverend Owen Lovejoy was selected to open the convention with prayer.[2]

The report of the proceedings of the convention in the newspapers of the time was meagre and inadequate.[3] It was published in pamphlet soon after the convention had adjourned, but covered only a few pages, being a mere skeleton of what happened and is even less satisfactory than the newspaper reports, because it gives the reader no conception of the spirit and character of the gathering. No roll of the members was

[1] Rhodes, *History of the United States,* II, 118.

[2] *Proceedings of the First Three Republican National Conventions, including Proceedings of the antecedent National Convention held at Pittsburg,* published by order of the Republican National Convention of 1892.

[3] *E. g.* Horace Greeley's report to the New York *Tribune,* February 21st and 22nd, 1856.

preserved, and the several histories of political parties and conventions which have since appeared, contain little more than a mere reference to the subject. Mr. George W. Julian has written admirably about this early Republican gathering in the American Historical Review,[1] and was officially and somewhat actively connected with its proceedings.

An exhaustive search of the records and a close examination of the Pittsburg papers, published at that time, revealed about 260 persons who were members of the convention; there may have been more, if so, their names were not recorded by themselves nor were they noted by others and in 1906 there were apparently but ten survivors.[2] A contemporary writer, however, estimated the number who attended at from three to four hundred.[3]

Ohio, New York and Pennsylvania sent the largest contingents to the convention but around this nucleus were gathered small but earnest delegations representing twenty-eight States and Territories, not only the free States but also Maryland, Virginia, South Carolina and Missouri.[4]

It was not a convention of delegates selected by constitutent assemblies of the people but a mass conven-

---

[1] *American Historical Review,* IV, 313.

[2] Address of William Barnes, Sr., delivered at the Golden Jubilee of the Republican Party, Philadelphia, June 17, 1906 (Published by A. B. Burk, Philadelphia, 1906).

[3] B. F. Hall, *The Republican Party,* 446-460 (1856).

[4] A good contemporary account is found in B. F. Hall, *The Republican Party,* 446-460 (1856).

tion of men, "self-appointed delegates," [1] who favored
the formation of a great national anti-slavery-extension
party and volunteered their services in the undertak-
ing. Though appearing from different States, the so-
called delegates at the Pittsburg convention represented
no one save themselves.[2] "Its members came together
in the dead of winter when no candidates were to be
nominated and no offices were to be divided. Probably
a majority of them had passed the meridian of life,
but all seemed equally in earnest and absorbed in their
work. The great body of the members had never devoted themselves to the business of politics. They
were building better than they knew."[2] The convention was in session two days and its purpose was fully
accomplished. Radicals and men of conservative type
were there—Giddings and Lovejoy, Julian of Indiana,
Chandler of Michigan and King of New York.

The convention assembled at 11 o'clock in Lafayette
Hall. It was called to order by Hon. Lawrence Brainerd of Vermont, who read the call upon which it had
convened and asked John A. King of New York, a son
of Rufus King, to act as temporary chairman. After
brief and appropriate remarks Mr. King called on the

[1] Addison B. Burk, in an address at the Golden Jubilee of the
Republican party at Philadelphia, June 17th, 1906, says: "The Pittsburg convention was a meeting of self-appointed delegates seeking
to found a new party." * * * * * * *
"This was the most spontaneous convention in the history of
American politics. The delegates were not chosen by any settled
rule. * * * The delegates met as delegates of the same party
for the first time and most of them were unknown to each other.
* * * The party was young, it was a young men's party and a
young men's convention."

[2] Julian, *American Historical Review*, IV, 313, *supra*, page 30.

Reverend Owen Lovejoy, who was present as a representative from Illinois, to open the proceedings with prayer.[1]

A committee on permanent organization, consisting of one member from each State and Territory, was then appointed by the chairman, and while it was engaged in its work in an adjoining room, the assemblage listened to the speeches of Horace Greeley, Lovejoy and Giddings.

This differed from the method subsequently adopted for the appointment of the committee on permanent organization in Republican national conventions, which, as we shall see later, consisted of one delegate from each State and Territory, selected by the several delegations respectively.[2]

A resolution was adopted that a committee of one delegate from each State, Territory and the District of Columbia be appointed to draw up an address and resolutions for the consideration of the convention and that a similar committee on national organization be formed.

Of the first day's meeting, Horace Greeley said in the New York *Tribune*[3]: "The Republican convention has completed its first day's session and has accomplished much to cement former political differences and distinctions and to mark the inauguration of a National party based upon the principle of freedom. The gather-

[1] The name of Lovejoy was an inspiration for it recalled the murder of his brother by a mob at Alton, in 1837 for merely exercising his Constitutional right of free speech in a free State in talking about slavery.

[2] See *infra,* page 67.

[3] New York *Tribune,* Feb. 23, 1856.

ing is very large and the enthusiasm is unbounded. It combines much character and talent with integrity of purpose and devotion to the great principles which underlie our government; its moral and political effect on the country will be felt for the next quarter of a century * * * The day has been principally occupied by the committees in preparing their reports, and by the delegates in committee of the whole in listening to speeches from eminent gentlemen who represent the several States. The business of perfecting a National organization will come up to-morrow forenoon. Adjourned."

Greeley's reports,[1] sent by magnetic telegraph to the New York *Tribune,* gave to the Pittsburg convention or meeting factitious importance and by this means greatly helped, by adding to its dignity and importance, to prepare the way for a real organization of the new party at Philadelphia in the following June.[2] Referring to these dispatches in an address delivered at the Golden Jubilee celebration of the Republican party in Philadelphia, June 17th, 1906, Mr. Addison B. Burk called them the "successful efforts to boost a cause that at the time needed artifical stimulation."

The usual parliamentary routine was followed on the second day. The convention met at 9 o'clock; the several committees not being ready to report, time was occupied in listening to ten minute speeches by representatives of the different States, giving an account of

[1] *Vide,* also the dispatches of Feb. 21 and 22, 1856, from Pittsburg to the N. Y. *Tribune* of those dates.

[2] Leslie's *History of the Republican Party,* Chapters I and II; G. O. Seilhaimer.

the progress of free principles in the various sections of the Union.

Simeon Draper for the committee on organization, reported the permanent officers of the convention: for president, Francis P. Blair of Maryland, and for vice-presidents, one from each State and Territory represented.

The committee on national organization, consisting of one member from each State and Territory was appointed by the chairman and this committee through its chairman Mr. George W. Julian recommended to the assembly the holding of a Republican national convention for the nomination of candidates for President and Vice-President at Philadelphia on the 17th of June (the anniversary of the battle of Bunker Hill), to consist of delegates from each State double the number of its representation in Congress, (following the model of the other party conventions[1]). The committee also proposed that the Republicans of each State be recommended to complete their organization at the earliest moment by the appointment of State, county and district committees and the formation of clubs in every town and township throughout the land.

The appointment of a national executive committee to consist of one member from each State represented in the convention and one from the District of Columbia and one from Kansas, with Morgan of New York as chairman, and Banks, Chase, Wilmot and Blair among

---

[1] In the Anti-Masonic convention of 1831, the first regularly constituted national nominating convention ever held in this country congressional representation was taken as the rule of party presentation and furnished a precedent for all subsequent conventions.

its members, was also recommended by the committee on national organization.[1]

The report of the committee on national organization further recommended that the national executive committee be authorized to add to their number one member from each State not represented and to fill vacancies.[2] The recommendation with regard to the proposed national convention was on motion of Mr. Lovejoy amended so as to make the delegates to the national convention consist of three from each Congressional district. "The report of the committee on national organization, as thus amended, was adopted and the national Republican party became a fact."[3]

This committee on national organization was a novelty in national conventions. It was formed to meet the peculiar necessities of the case and its function was to get the party under weigh nationally. Having accomplished this it ceased to exist and no similar committee has ever been appointed in any subsequent Republican national convention. It was not the forerunner of the present Republican national committee. This we find rather in the national executive committee, the formation of which the committee on national organization recommended, for it was this executive committee which, as we shall see, issued the call for the first Republican national convention, and generally assumed the duties of a national committee.

[1] *American Historical Review,* IV, 319 (G. W. Julian), *supra.*

[2] The details of the proceedings in the convention are found in *Proceedings of the First Three Republican National Conventions including Proceedings of the antecedent National Convention held at Pittsburg* as compiled by Charles W. Johnson, Secretary of the convention of 1892.

[3] *American Historical Review,* IV, 320 (G. W. Julian).

The executive committee, organized at the Pittsburg gathering to take charge of the national convention, represented twenty-one States and Territories and the District of Columbia. The formation of this committee with a view to perfecting the national organization was the main purpose of the gathering and the most important thing accomplished.

A stirring address [1] to the country stating the principles and purposes of the Republican party, as reported by Mr. Mann of New York from the committee on address and resolutions, was also unanimously adopted and put forth by the convention. The repeal of all laws allowing the introduction of slavery into territory now free, the support of the citizens of Kansas in their resistance to the invading slave-holders, the immediate admission of Kansas to the Union as a free State, and the opposition to and overthrow of the national administration which "has shown itself to be weak and faithless and * * * identified with the progress of the slave power to national supremacy," were declared to be the objects for which unity in political action were sought.

The address to the country or platform also concluded with a sort of "call" for a convention to select

[1] The document was written by Henry J. Raymond, Lieutenant-Governor of New York and is printed in full in Raymond & Maverick, *New York Journalism;* also in part in Rhodes, *History of the United States,* II, 118-119, and in Hall, *The Republican party,* 446 (1856). The paper is called "Address of the first Republican National Convention held at Pittsburg, Pa., February 22nd, 1856. Declarations of Principles and Purposes which we seek to promote." It consists of eleven closely printed pages and an original printed copy is to be found in the Mercantile Library of the City of New York.

presidential nominees which doubtless served as a model for the call which was issued March 29th, 1856.[1]

A motion that the proceedings be printed in pamphlet form and circulated was approved. A vote of thanks to the officers of the convention and the citizens of Pittsburg was carried and the convention adjourned *sine die.*

The national executive committee, appointed by the convention of February 22nd, met in Washington on March 27th 1856 and after a prolonged discussion issued the following call:[2]

To the People of the United States:

The People of the United States without regard to past political differences or divisions, who are opposed to the repeal of the Missouri Compromise, to the policy of the present Administration, to the extension of Slavery into the Territories, in favor of the admission of Kansas as a free State and of restoring the action of the Federal Government, to the principles of Washington and Jefferson, are invited by the National Committee appointed by the Pittsburg Convention of the 22nd of February, 1856, to send from each State, three delegates from each congressional district, and six delegates at large, to meet in Philadelphia on the 17th of June next for the purpose of recommending candidates to be supported for the offices of President and Vice-President of the United States.

E. D. MORGAN, N. Y.	FRANCIS P. BLAIR, Md.
A. P. STONE, Ohio.	W. M. CHASE, R. I.
J. M. NILES, Conn.	DAVID WILMOT, Penn.

[1] B. F. Hall, *The Republican Party,* 446-460 (1856).

[2] So important was the wording of that call in view of the desire not to offend any one and draw in from the ranks of all parties that two days were spent in session at Willard's Hotel in preparing the call for the nominating convention. (*Official Proceedings of the first*

J. Z. GOODRICH, Mass.

A. R. HALLOWELL, Me.

CHARLES DICKIE, Mich.

LAWRENCE BRAINERD, Vt.

E. D. WILLIAMS, Del.

G. G. FOGG, N. H.

W. GROSE, Ind.

JOHN G. FEE, Ky.

GEORGE RYE, Va.

E. S. LELAND, Ill.

A. J. STEVENS, Ia.

WYMAN SPOONER, Wis.

JAMES REDPATH, Mo.

CORNELIUS COLE, Cal.

C. M. K. PAULISON, N. J.

LEWIS CLEPHANE, D. C.

National Committee.

Dated, Washington, March 29th, 1856.

In issuing a formal call to the people of the United States, the "National Executive Committee" followed the instructions of the Pittsburg convention as to the number of delegates to be sent by each State and then assumed the prerogative, in the call, of fixing the date and place for the holding of the next national convention of the party. This practice of issuing a call, specifying the date, place and composition of the succeeding national convention has been followed by the national committee of the Republican party ever since.

Pursuant to the call of the national executive committee above set forth, the delegates elected to the first Republican national nominating convention ever held, assembled in Musical Fund Hall in the City of Philadelphia, on Tuesday, June 17th, 1856, at 11 o'clock in the forenoon.[1] Each State had a representation in the convention equal to three times its electoral vote.

three Republican National Conventions, published in 1892, by order of the Republican National Convention of that year by Charles W. Johnson, its Secretary, page 14.)

[1] A Golden Jubilee was held there 50 years later, June 17th, 1906; 300 veterans of the Fremont campaign were present. The proceedings were published at Philadelphia by Addison B. Burk in 1906. (See footnote to page 16, *supra*.)

Five hundred and sixty-five delegates[1] were found to be
present,—old Whigs, Wilmot-Proviso Democrats and
Free-Soilers,—representing every free State and Delaware, Kentucky, Maryland and Virginia, the Territories
of Minnesota, (Nebraska)[2] and Kansas and the District
of Columbia. As many delegates as wished to represent any State were appointed, but the vote of each
State was restricted as specified in the call.[3] The
party, then in its infancy, "was glad to take anyone
who could go." [4]

State conventions composed of delegates selected
by party voters afforded the model for a national convention. As early as 1831, in Baltimore, the Anti-
Masonic convention brought together 112 delegates
from a large number of States in the Union; and in December of that year the Whig party, at its convention
at the City of Baltimore, boasted of 156 delegates, representing 18 States and the District of Columbia.[5] The
delegates to these early conventions were chosen in a
variety of ways and it was many years before each

[1] Curtis, *The Republican Party,* I, page 255.

[2] Though it has sometimes been said that the Territory of Nebraska
was represented yet the records of the convention contain no mention
of the delegates from that State as voting or participating in the
convention.

[3] The Territory of Kansas, not having any electoral vote, was given
9 votes in the convention. Thus at this early stage the Republican
party showed its liberal policy toward Territories, which has been
continued to the present time.

[4] Statement of the late Mr. Cephas Brainerd to the writer.

[5] *Journal of the National Republican Convention which assembled
at the City of Baltimore, December 10th, 1831, for the nomination
of Candidates to fill the offices of President and Vice-President.*

party was so completely organized down to the election district or precinct as to secure regularity in the choice of delegates. "In the earlier period, it seems, the delegates to the national convention were sometimes chosen by State conventions, sometimes by legislative caucuses and district conventions and sometimes by local mass meetings of the voters. Even as late as 1864 some of the delegates to the Republican or Union national convention were selected by legislative causes." [1]

In May, 1838, the Whig State convention in Ohio, after a warm discussion, decided by a large majority that each congressional district should have the right to choose its delegates to the national convention, the two delegates-at-large being chosen as before by the State convention, "as being most democratic and best calculated to bring out the real sentiment of the people." [2] This method of choosing delegates which is by far the fairest, has from that time to this steadily gained in favor, until it is to-day the more popular method throughout the country. The Republican party, as we shall see, by a rule adopted at the national convention of 1884, compelled every State to choose its delegates in that manner. In the Democratic party however in some of the States all the delegates are still chosen by the State convention.

The early conventions of the Republican party, State and national, were to a large extent mass meetings rather than representative bodies. This was especially

[1] C. A. Beard, *American Government and Politics,* 132.

[2] F. W. Dallinger, *Nominations for Elective Office,* 43 and Niles' Register, LVI, 259 (cited by Dallinger).

true of the Pittsburg convention of 1856 and also, as we shall see, of the Philadelphia convention.[1]

No uniform rule was adopted in electing delegates to the latter convention of 1856, nor were they chosen by means of complicated party machinery.[2] The method of selection was left entirely to the states, which selected any one of the various methods above enumerated. In some cases even the so-called delegates volunteered their services and the appointment was ratified by a State convention afterwards. Most of the members had no form of credentials. No rule had been provided in the call securing uniformity as to the number of votes to which each State should be entitled. Only the number of delegates for each had been determined upon. In this respect, the early Republican conventions contrasted greatly with the later regularly constituted representative bodies, composed exclusively of delegates each of whom has been duly chosen according to recognized party methods in his own State and has been furnished with the proper credentials.

No reference was made in the call to the sending of delegates by the Territories and the District of Columbia, but in spite of that fact the Territories of Minnesota, (Nebraska)[3] and Kansas and the District of Columbia sent delegates who were admitted.

Credentials were not scrutinized and apparently every delegate who applied was admitted without question, so that there was the greatest discrepancy in

[1] So also was the seceding Republican convention which met at Cincinnati in 1872 and nominated Greeley. Bryce, *American Commonwealth*, II, 145.

[2] Rhodes, *History of the United States, II,* 182.

[3] See Note 2 to page 39.

representation,[1]—New York, for example, having 96 delegates, Pennsylvania 81 and Ohio 69. Many of the more remote States were unrepresented and altogether there were only 565 delegates present. As a result of this inequality, the convention was forced to adopt a rule fixing the number of votes to which each State was entitled.[2]

Alexander K. McClure was a Pennsylvania delegate to the Philadelphia convention.[3] He refers to this assembly as a mass convention, similar to a State convention, held at Pittsburg, which he had attended the year previously. He says it was composed of a loose aggregation of political free-thinkers as the party had no organization and the States sent large or small delegations, as was most convenient. Mr. McClure was so much dissatisfied with the radical Republican attitude adopted by the convention, that, though he attended its first session, he did not enroll as a delegate and did not participate after the first session.

The Philadelphia convention was called to order by Hon. Edwin D. Morgan of New York, chairman of the Republican national committee,[4] setting a precedent which has been followed in the succeeding Republican national conventions. On behalf of the national committee, he nominated Hon. Robert Emmet of New York for temporary president of the convention and the question being taken on the nomination it was re-

---

[1] A. K. McClure, *Our Presidents and How We Make Them,* 158.
[2] See *infra,* page 46.
[3] A. K. McClure, *Our Presidents and How We Make Them,* 136, 137·
[4] The national executive committee, appointed by the Pittsburg convention called itself merely the national committee. See opening address of Mr. Morgan quoted in part at page 205 *infra.*

sponded to by a unanimous "aye," and Mr. Emmet was conducted to the chair by two delegates appointed by Mr. Morgan. Mr. George G. Fogg of New Hampshire and Mr. Thomas G. Mitchell of Ohio were, on motion, appointed temporary secretaries of the convention,[1] Thus began the practice, now well settled in the Republican party conventions, of having the national committee name the temporary chairman as well as other temporary officers, who, unless there be opposition in the convention, become without question the temporary officers of the convention.[2]

The first problem coming before a national convention is the appointment of committees on credentials, rules, platform, and permanent organization. In the matter of credentials and rules, the resolution of Mr. A. P. Stone of Ohio (vesting the two functions in one committee) was carried as follows:

Resolved: That a committee, consisting of one delegate from each State and Territory represented in this Convention be selected by the delegates thereof who shall act as a Committee on Credentials, Rules and Appointments and report the number, names [sic] and post-office address of each delegate together with rules for the government of the Convention.[3]

[1] The details of the proceedings of the convention are found in *Proceedings of the first Three Republican National Conventions* as compiled by Charles W. Johnson, Secretary of the convention of 1892 (Minneapolis, Minn.).

[2] This right was first questioned in the convention of 1884, see *infra*, p. 120.

[3] This practice of a joint committee for credentials as well as rules has not been adhered to since that time in Republican national conventions, thereafter a separate committee was appointed for each.

In the matter of the preparation of a platform, the convention carried a resolution, offered by David Wilmot of Pennsylvania and amended by B. B. French of the District of Columbia, as follows:

Resolved: That a committee of one from each State and Territory represented be appointed to prepare and report for the action of the Convention, a platform of principles to be submitted to the people of the United States; that the member from each State and Territory represented be named by the delegates thereof; and that all resolutions or papers offered in the Convention in relation to such platform be referred to the committee thus appointed without debate.[1]

Resolved: That the said committee be requested to report at the earliest practicable moment and that no ballot be taken for President or Vice-President until after the platform is reported and adopted by the Convention.[2]

In the matter of a permanent organization the resolution of Mr. F. D. Kimball of Ohio was carried:

Resolved: That a committee of one from each State and Territory represented be selected by the several delegations to report officers to this Convention for its permanent organization.[3]

---

[1] This practice has been adhered to in Republican national conventions.

[2] This is now and has been ever since a part of the rules of every Republican national convention reported to each convention by its committee on rules and order of business.

[3] This practice has been adhered to in Republican national conventions.

A custom, which has prevailed in all Republican national conventions since the first one, was then sanctioned in the resolution offered by the same Ohio delegate, which was carried as follows:

Resolved: That the daily meetings of this Convention be opened with prayer, and that the officers of the Convention make the necessary arrangements to that effect by invitations to the clergymen of the city.[1]

The committee on permanent organization, which had been selected pursuant to the resolution quoted above, reported the following list of officers for the convention: president, Col. Henry S. Lane of Indiana, and a vice-president and secretary from each State and Territory represented.

The problem of selecting a national committee to call the convention of four years hence was met by the resolution of Mr. Kimball of Ohio, and was carried during the first day's proceedings as follows (but later reconsidered[2]):

Resolved: That a committee of one from each State and Territory represented in this Convention be appointed by the several delegations respectively to report the name of one person from each State and Territory to constitute the Republican National Committee for the ensuing four years,—such committee, when appointed, to elect their own chairman.[3]

---

[1] This has become a fixed custom in all succeeding national conventions without the adoption of a specific resolution.

[2] See *infra,* page 47.

[3] This practice has been adhered to ever since.

Owing to the fact noted above, that several States sent more than the quota of delegates to which the call entitled them, it became necessary for the convention to decide upon a plan of fixing the number of votes which each State should be authorized to cast in the convention and the method of giving such vote. To meet this question the Hon. Elbridge G. Spaulding from the committee on credentials and on rules for the government of the convention presented the following report, in part, which was adopted:

Resolved: That in voting for a candidate for President, the States be called in their order and that the chairman of each delegation present the number of votes given to each candidate for President by the delegates from his State, each State being limited in its votes to three times the number of electors to which such State is entitled: *Provided* that no State shall give a larger vote than the number of delegates actually present in the Convention;[1]

And provided: That Kansas shall be considered for this purpose as a State with the same electoral vote as any other State entitled to only one representative in Congress.

Resolved: That the same rule shall apply to the nomination of Vice-President.

They then considered the subject of the general rules of procedure and passed the following resolution, reported by the committee on rules:

Resolved: That the rules of the House of Representa-

---

[1] This with modifications and changes has been embodied in the rules of each succeeding national convention reported to it by its committee on rules and order of business.

tives be adopted so far as they are applicable to this Convention.[1]

In forming the national committee, the convention at the beginning of the second day's proceedings, reconsidered the resolution, adopted the previous day, and carried the resolution of Mr. Roland G. Hazard of Rhode Island, thus setting a precedent, as to the method of selecting the national party committee, which has been followed down to the present day by the Republican party:

Resolved: That the resolution adopted yesterday providing for the appointment of a committee to report to the Convention the names of the Republican National Committee for the next four years be, and the same hereby is reconsidered and that the said resolution be amended so as to read as follows:—

Resolved: That the several State and Territorial Delegations, through their chairmen report to the Convention the name of one citizen from their respective States and Territories to be a member of the Republican National Committee for the next four years and that the gentlemen so appointed constitute such Republican National Committee and that they elect the chairman of the Committee.[2]

The roll of members of the convention with their post-office addresses was read and each State was given the right to designate a member for the Republican national committee for the next four years. The list of

[1] This practice has been adhered to ever since in Republican national conventions with one exception, 1884.

[2] This practice has been followed in Republican national conventions, but see *infra*, Chapter IV.

names of the committee was then read to the convention.

The Hon. David Wilmot, chairman of the committee appointed the day before to prepare and report for the action of the convention a platform of principles to be submitted to the people of the United States, reported a preamble and series of resolutions to constitute such platform.[1]

Its leading points [2] were the denial of the authority of Congress, of a territorial legislature, of any individual or association of individuals to give legal existence to slavery in any Territory of the United States and the assertion of the "right and duty of Congress to prohibit in the Territories those twin relics of barbarism,—polygamy and slavery." The immediate admission of Kansas as a free State was demanded; appropriations by Congress for internal improvements [3] were recommended, and the restoration of the action of

[1] B. F. Hall, *The Republican Party*, 462 (1856). The full text of the platform may be found in Charles W. Johnson's *Proceedings of the First Three Republican National Conventions* published by order of the convention of 1892 through Mr. Johnson, who was the secretary of that convention, and also in Curtis, *The Republican Party*, I, 257. See also, the contemporary campaign text book, entitled "A Republican Edition for the Million" (1856), the first Republican national campaign text book ever issued, a photographic reprint of the title page of which forms the frontispiece of this volume. See also Stanwood's *History of Presidential Elections*, 205.

[2] The platform of 1856 bears a striking resemblance to the Declaration of the Anti-Slavery convention assembled in Philadelphia, December, 1833. An original printed copy of that declaration is on file in the Archives of the Nantucket Historical Society and has been reprinted in A. B. Burk, *Golden Jubilee of the Republican Party* (1906).

[3] Due to the Whig element in the party; see *infra*, page 164.

the Federal government to the principles of Washington and Jefferson was urged.

A committee of three was appointed by the chair in accordance with the report of the committee on resolutions "to address all parties of the country, with a view to elucidate the principles of action, and to conciliate them to the great object to which the labors of the convention had been devoted."

A motion to proceed to the nomination of President was debated for some time, and during the discussion it was brought out that the New York delegates were unanimously for the nomination of William H. Seward, but that he had requested the withdrawal of his name; in a letter Judge McLean declined the use of his name as a candidate, but at the request of Pennsylvania, New Jersey and Ohio, it was placed before the convention [1]; and a letter was presented from Salmon P. Chase containing the request that his name be withheld from the convention.[2] The president then declared that the business of the convention was to proceed to the nomination of a Republican candidate for President of the United States and that, pursuant to the resolution of Mr. John E. Seeley of New York adopted at the morning session, the convention should proceed to "take an informal ballot for a candidate for President of the United States." This taking of an informal ballot served merely as a means of making nominations since the names of no candidate had been

[1] Rhodes, *History of the United States,* II, 184. Also New York *Evening Post,* New York *Times* and New York *Tribune,* June 19th, 1856. Bigelow's *Life of Fremont.*

[2] *Ibid.*

formally presented to the convention. The practice was never again followed in Republican conventions.

Two tellers were appointed by the chair and the vote was then taken in accordance with the recommendation of the committee on rules, which had been passed the previous day. The States were called in geographical order,[1] and the chairman of each delegation presented the number of votes given to each candidate for President by the delegates from his State. The sum of the votes was announced by the tellers amid cheers, as follows: on the first ballot for a candidate for President, for John C. Fremont of California, 359 votes; for John McLean of Ohio, 190 votes; for Nathaniel P. Banks of Massachusetts, 1 vote; for Charles Sumner of Massachusetts, 2 votes; and for William H. Seward of New York, 1 vote.

The motion of General J. W. Webb of New York was then adopted that this convention do immediately proceed to "take a formal vote for a Republican candidate for President of the United States." On the formal ballot taken in the same manner as the informal one, Fremont received all but 38 votes.

General Webb then offered a resolution that John C. Fremont of California be unanimously nominated by this convention by acclamation as the Republican candidate for President of the United States.

The resolution of General James W. Webb, that

[1] This differed from the method adopted in later Republican conventions of calling the States in alphabetical order (see *infra,* page 171) but followed the practice of the National Republican or Whig party in 1831.

Fremont's nomination be made unanimous,[1] created a precedent which has been followed without exception in the Republican national conventions from that day with respect to the nominations for President of the United States.

That resolution was adopted and the convention then immediately proceeded to "take an informal vote for a candidate for Vice-President of the United States to be supported by the Republican party at the ensuing election." [2]

A similar method of voting to that employed in the balloting for President was used in the informal and formal ballot for candidate for Vice-President.

William L. Dayton of New Jersey received 259 votes; Abraham Lincoln of Illinois 110; Nathaniel P Banks of Massachusetts 46; David Wilmot of Penn-sylvania 43; Charles Sumner of Massachusetts 35, and 53 were scattering, and on the formal ballot Day-ton was unanimously nominated. Dayton's nomination was the Whig share of the result.

A resolution was then offered and passed that a "National Convention of young men in favor of Free Speech, Free Soil and Free Kansas, and of Fremont for President of the United States be held in the month of September, 1856, in the City of Harrisburg, in the State of Pennsylvania, under the call of the Republican National Committee."

Judge Hoar of Massachusetts called up the resolution to hold the next national convention at Cleveland,

[1] This followed the familiar practice of the National Republican and Whig conventions

[2] See *infra,* page 174

which had been previously made and tabled, and moved its reference to the Republican national committee. He thought that the committee should name the place.

After this problem had been discussed at length,[1] the convention voted to leave the question to be determined by the national committee. This was the origin of a precedent which has been followed by the Republican party ever since that day, with interesting results.[2] In course of time, the entire business preliminary to the convention came to be entrusted to the Republican national committee, which is discussed in a subsequent chapter.

The chairman of the convention appointed a committee of nine delegates with himself as the tenth to notify the nominees of the action of the convention.[3]

A resolution of thanks by the convention to its vice-presidents and secretaries for their ability and fidelity in the discharge of their duties was then carried as was also a resolution of thanks to the citizens of Philadelphia for their kindness and hospitality shown to the delegates during the session of the convention. This practice has likewise been followed, from that day as the concluding ceremony of the great national party conclave.

[1] The reason advanced by Judge Hoar was that "if successful in the coming election they might hold their next Convention in Kentucky or Virginia." Massachusetts desired to advance the column to the South, holding their party to be a national party; therefore a decision at present was inadvisable (*Official Proceedings of the Convention of 1856*, p. 81).

[2] See *infra*, Chapter IV.

[3] Leslie's *History of the Republican Party*, I, p. 77 (G. O. Seilhaimer).

The convention, on resolution, then adjourned *sine die.*

Although the first national convention of the Republican party ordered its minutes to be published in pamphlet form, yet from some cause or other it was not done and the newspapers of that time contain a very meagre account of its proceedings.

On the 19th of June, the day following the date of the nominations, Colonel Lane, the president of the convention and the committee associated with him for the purpose, addressed letters to the nominees respectively informing them of their unanimous nominations and requesting them in behalf of the convention to accept the same. In response they received letters of acceptance from the candidates.[1]

This practice of notifying the candidates has obtained without exception down to the present day, although in subsequent years, in addition to a formal letter directed to the nominee and delivered by the committee, an elaborate address has been made to the candidate at his home by the chairman or some particularly representative man on the committee. Moreover, the letters of acceptance, which in the early days of the party were short and merely thanked the convention for the honor conferred, became in subsequent years, in many instances, rather lengthy documents and formed, in a way, second platforms.[2]

At a meeting of the national Republican committee at the Girard Hotel, after the termination of the con-

---

[1] These are published in the *Republican Scrap Book* (Boston, 1856), and in B. F. Hall, *The Republican party,* 465-471 (1856).

[2] For a fuller discussion see *infra,* page 186.

vention, Edwin D. Morgan was chosen chairman and
N. B. Judd, secretary. Apparently no treasurer was
chosen.

It has become an established custom in the party
that the national committee should meet shortly after
the conclusion of the convention and organize by the
choice of a chairman and secretary. In later years, as
we shall see, it also elected at or about that time a
treasurer and other officers, together with an executive
committee.

In the election of 1856 the Democratic candidates
were successful; the votes stood:

	Popular Vote.	Electoral Vote.
James Buchanan	1,838,169	174
John C. Fremont,	1,341,264	114
Millard Fillmore	874,534	8 (Md.)

It was a show of strength,[1] most gratifying to the
Republicans and was beyond measure startling. They
carried every Northern State but Pennsylvania, New
Jersey, Indiana and Illinois, and "gained portentous
strength" even in those States. Their defeat was such
a narrow one that the votes of Illinois and Pennsylvania would have made Fremont President. It is note-
worthy that in 1860, provision was made for both these
latter States, for the former, by Lincoln's nomination,
and for the latter, by the protective tariff clause in the
platform. In the West, the Republicans were practically the only party which disputed supremacy with

[1] In New York State Fremont received 276,007 votes (Rhodes, *History of the United States,* II, 185.)

the Democrats, and thereafter they were to be the only powerful party standing face to face with the Democrats in the East. The Know-Nothings and Whigs vanished from the field of national politics. Parties were to be thenceforth compact and sectional. "We have lost a battle," was the comment of the New York *Tribune,* on the day after the election, "the Bunker Hill of the new struggle for freedom is past; the Saratoga and Yorktown are yet to be achieved," and Whittier expressed the general feeling in the words, "If months have well-nigh won the field, what may not four years do?"

In order to realize their ideals it was of course necessary for the Republicans to secure both Houses of Congress and the Presidency. This was rendered possible by the Democratic disruption, the presence of four tickets in the field, and the nomination of Abraham Lincoln in 1860.

In the meantime, the United States Supreme Court rendered the decision in the case of Dred Scott. This marked the last attempt to decide the contest between slavery extension and slavery restriction by forms of law, and from this time, the course of events tended with increasing rapidity to a settlement by force. The first compromise (in 1820) had prohibited slavery in part of the Territories, leaving the question open as to the remainder. The next Compromise Measures (in 1850), as interpreted in the Kansas-Nebraska Act of 1854, had opened all the Territories to slavery, if established by popular sovereignty. But the Dred Scott decision in its logical consequences, opened all the Territories and possibly the Free States to at least a temporary establishment of slavery, wherever a slave owner might see fit to carry his slave. It was plain that this would never be accepted as law by the Free States. The results of the decision therefore, were to show the failure of the Supreme Court as an arbiter and to call the attention of the North to the wholly impossible demands of the slave power.

A meeting of the Republican members of Congress at Washington on the 7th of December, 1857, unanimously adopted the following resolution:

Resolved: That we, the Republican members of the House, deem this a proper occasion to reaffirm our adherence to the principles announced by the Republican National Convention, held at Philadelphia, in June, 1856, and we will continue our opposition to any administration that does not practically enforce those doctrines; that we will resist by all constitutional means the recent attempt of the Judicial and Executive Departments of the Government to nationalize the sectional institution of slavery; that we regard the acts in Kansas of the present and the last National administrations as a continued series of frauds and outrages now attempted to be culminated by forcing upon the people of that territory a state constitution, framed by persons not elected by them, one which was not submitted to them and is known to be offensive to a great majority of them and made in direct violation even of their own repeated and solemn pledges that the people should be permitted to form and regulate their own institutions, in their own way. We will resist such outrages upon popular rights and in doing so invoke the support of the people of the United States without distinction of party.

In the summer and fall of 1857 the prospects of the Republican party did not seem bright; there was a natural reaction from the high enthusiasm which had characterized the campaign of the preceding year. In the Northwest, the outlook for the new party was especially gloomy. The result of the fall elections all over the North was discouraging. A large falling off of the Republican vote was noted nearly everywhere, due to apathy and the fact that the financial stringency engrossed public attention. The congressional elections of that year were so unfavorable that there were but 92 Republicans out of 237 members in the Congress of 1857-59.

But in 1858 the outlook was far more promising. New England was a solid phalanx under the Republican banner. Northwestern States like Ohio, Iowa, Indiana and Michigan were winning over the doubters in the Democratic party, and in New York, against a desperate fusion of anti-Republicans, the Republicans elected Edwin D. Morgan for Governor, by a plurality of over 17,000.

Pennsylvania [1] elected an anti-administration ticket of State officers by more than 20,000 majority, and "resolutely turned its back upon the South, whose faithful handmaid it had been for full three-score years."

The contest in Illinois was extremely bitter, and of singular interest, and later events made it historical. Here Stephen A. Douglas canvassed for re-election to the United States Senate and had been nominated by the Democrats. Against him the Republican State convention meeting at Springfield, on

[1] Buchanan's own State.

June 16, 1858, put Abraham Lincoln in nomination **for** senatorial succession.[1]

The Republicans did not obtain a majority in the Illinois legislature, but Douglas went back to the Senate weakened in prestige and with loss of authority.

The elections of the Autumn, taking the country as a whole, were most favorable to the Republicans. Morgan as we have seen was elected in New York by a large majority; a Republican legislature was chosen and all the members of Congress elected, except four, were Republicans or anti-Lecompton men.[2]   Among them were Reuben E. Fenton, Roscoe Conkling and Francis E. Spinner.   At this election Pennsylvania, New Jersey and Minnesota for the first time gave Republican majorities.   Every New England State elected a Republican governor, as well as Ohio, Pennsylvania and Iowa; Michigan and Wisconsin increased their Republican vote; the Indiana Republicans elected a majority of the congressional delegation from that State and the Republicans were generally successful throughout the North.

If we except Illinois, where, as we have seen, a Douglas legislature was elected, although the State gave a Republican majority on the popular vote, only California, of the free States, voted in favor of the administration, and Oregon, which had not as yet been admitted, voted as California did.   On May 11

---

[1] Lincoln addressed the delegates at this convention in the most carefully prepared speech he had ever made, dwelling on his favorite doctrine that a house divided against itself cannot stand.

[2] *I. e.*   Men opposed to Buchanan's scheme of forcing a slavery constitution on Kansas.

of that year, Minnesota had been admitted to the Union as a State with a constitution that forbade slavery and she at once joined the Republican column.

In the Spring of 1859, sharp debates and discussions were the order of the day in the Senate. The Democratic party was seen to be steadily dividing into two camps, and the convention of 1860 was looked forward to by the Democrats with no little foreboding. The Republican party on the contrary seemed to be more firmly cemented than ever and to be daily gaining strength, particularly in the Middle West.[1]

The Thirty-sixth Congress met in Washington, December 5, 1859. The Republican minority in the Senate now numbered 24 or 25, while in the House of Representatives the Republicans totalled 113, Administration Democrats 93, anti-Lecompton Democrats 8, "South Americans"[2] 23. It will be seen that the anti-Slavery majority was five, though the Republican party as such had only a plurality.

Thus, during the four years which followed its first national convention, the Republican party steadily advanced. It found its most effective support among the Northern farmers who believed that slavery should be excluded from the great Western Territory in order that homesteads might be erected there by free men[3];

[1] The Oberlin affair, where a professor of the college and several students, besides other respectable citizens, were sent to jail and fined, because of the part taken in the rescue of a runaway slave, only served to intensify the anti-slavery extension feeling at the North, not only because of the Fugitive Slave Law, but of the system which made it possible.

[2] Southern members of the American or Know-Nothing party.

[3] C. A. Beard, *American Government and Politics,* 115.

and indeed it has been called "The Homestead Party" by an eminent publicist.[1] To the homestead element was added the manufacturing interest of the East which was clamoring for more protection against European competition.[2] "The alliance of these two great forces made a formidable party,—not an abolitionist party, but a homestead and protective tariff party standing for the exclusion of slavery from the territories."[3]

In recognition of the growing power and importance of the great West, the Republican national convention was called to meet in Chicago, on the 16th day of May, 1860. The former presidential canvass, though resulting in the defeat of Fremont, had nevertheless shown the remarkable popular strength of the Republican party in the country at large; since then its double victory in Congress against the Lecompton constitution and at the congressional elections over the representatives who supported this constitution, gave it confidence and aggressive activity. But the party now received new inspiration and impetus from the Charleston disruption on April 30th, 1860. Former possibility was suddenly changed to strong probability of success in the ensuing presidential election.

The Republican national convention met on May 16, 17 and 18, 1860, at Chicago, Illinois, in a wigwam [4] built for the occasion which it was said would ac-

[1] J. R. Commons, vol. XXIV, p. 468, *Political Science Quarterly,* Sept., 1909, Horace Greeley and the Republican Party.

[2] See Republican Platform of 1860.

[3] C. A. Beard, *American Government and Politics,* 116.

[4] The building called a wigwam was a temporary frame structure

commodate 10,000 people. All the free States and six slave States, Maryland, Delaware, Virginia, Kentucky, Missouri and Texas, the Territories of Kansas and Nebraska and the District of Columbia were represented in all by 466 delegates.[1]

The contrast between this gathering and the national convention of 1856 is worthy of remark. Then a hall accommodating 2000 was quite sufficient, now the wigwam holding five times that number "was jammed and twenty thousand people outside clamored for admittance;[2] then the wire-pullers looked askance at a

but admirably fitted for the occasion. Its acoustic qualities were perfect and every part of it could be seen from every other part. The name is still applied in Western cities by Republicans to buildings used for party purposes.

A good contemporary account of the convention of 1860 is given by Murat Halstead, who was present as correspondent for the Cincinnati *Commercial*. Referring to the wigwam, he says, "The City of Chicago is attending to this convention in magnificent style. It is a great place for great hotels and all have their capacity for accommodation tested. The great feature is the wigwam, erected in the past month, expressly for the use of the convention by the republicans of Chicago at the cost of $7,000. It is a small edition of the New York Crystal Palace built of boards and will hold ten thousand persons comfortably, and is admirable for its accoustic excellence. An ordinary voice can be heard through the whole structure with ease. * * * Vast as the wigwam is, not one-fifth of those who would be glad to get inside can be accommodated." (*National Political Conventions of 1860*, p. 121.) Only delegates and gentlemen visitors accompanied by ladies had seats. Spectators unaccompanied by ladies who had tickets of admission had to stand. In all Republican national conventions since, seats have been furnished for spectators.

[1] Rhodes, *History of the United States*, II, 456.

[2] It may safely be said that no other country provides in its party life for any gatherings comparable in size, interest and representative character, with our quadrennial national conventions.

movement whose success was problematical, now they hastened to identify themselves with a party that apparently had the game in its own hand."[1]   And "office-seekers, who, since 1858, had formed a noticeable part of the Republican organization,[2] were now present in numbers, for the purpose of making prominent their devotion to the party and its principles."   In 1856, the delegates were "liberty-loving enthusiasts and largely volunteers," now the delegates were "chosen by means of the organization peculiar to a powerful party and, in political wisdom, were the pick of the Republicans."

While the first Republican national convention presented a sort of extemporized gathering, the greater part of whose members had no form of credentials, the convention of 1860 was largely composed of regular delegations from the several States.   At that time the contest in which they were about to engage seemed but "a tentative effort and the leading men would not accept the nomination, while now, triumph appeared so certain, that, everyone of the master spirits was eager to be the candidate."   The most potent cause of this change, beside the continued growth of anti-slavery extension sentiment, was the split in the Democratic party, "which began with the refusal of Douglas to submit to Southern dictation."[3]

No convention had ever before attracted such a crowd of on-lookers. "By the second day of the convention, thirty or forty thousand strangers, mostly from

---

[1] Rhodes, *History of the United States,* II, 457.

[2] See *Lincoln-Douglas Debates,* page 230, cited in Rhodes, II, 457; also *Lincoln-Douglas Debates,* page 261 (Published by O. S. Hubbell & Co., Cleveland, Ohio, 1895).

[3] Rhodes, *History of the United States,* II, 457.

the Northwest, had flocked to the city eager to be associated with the great historic event that was promised and thinking perhaps to affect the result by their presence and shouts." [1] "Never before had there been such systematic efforts to create an opinion that the people demanded this or that candidate. Organized bodies of men were sent out day and night to make street demonstrations for their favorite or were collected to pack the audience room in the Convention Hall so that cheers might greet each mention of his name. These procedures were very different from those of similar Whig gatherings heretofore,"—the usually accepted Republican model,—which had been "marked by respectability and decorum." [2]

The writer was so fortunate as to be able to supplement the meagre historical accounts, at his disposal, with reference to the election of delegates to this convention, by a personal interview with General Stewart L. Woodford. General Woodford was an alternate to the Lincoln convention of 1860 from Fairfield County, Connecticut. The writer expressed his surprise at this, knowing that General Woodford was at that time a citizen of the State of New York and a resident of the City of New York. He was then informed that custom, in those early days, did not require the delegate to be a citizen of the State which he represented at the convention, nor did he have to be a resident of the district which sent him, as is usually the case at the present time.

[1] Nicolay and Hay, II, *Life of Lincoln,* 264; Halstead, *National Political Conventions,* 140. Rhodes, *History of the United States,* II, 456.

[2] Rhodes, *History of the United States,* II, 458.

The reason delegates were not required to be citizens of the State they represented in the early conventions was because the party was then in its infancy and there was no pay attached to the position, and on the other hand it involved considerable expense to the individual, so that a State organization was often only too glad to have anyone of prominence from any part of the United States volunteer to represent it in the convention. Accordingly, Connecticut, in recognition of certain political speeches which General Woodford had made during the previous campaign, nominated him as an alternate to the convention of 1860. General Woodford did not recall [1] the details as to the method by which he had been elected in Connecticut. He remembered that a State convention had been held and that the delegates there elected were authorized to appoint alternates and this was how he was chosen. His appointment bore the signature of A. Homer Byington,[2] editor of the Norwalk *Gazette,* of Norwalk, Con-

[1] General Woodford was likewise a regular delegate from the State of New York to the Republican convention of 1872 which nominated Grant for the second time. To the best of the General's recollection, the method of his election was as follows: A State convention was called, which elected the four delegates-at-large from New York and then the delegates to that convention got together and reported delegates from each district to the convention and then the convention ratified these men. This is exactly the method pursued by the Democratic party to-day for the election of delegates to the national convention.

[2] At the suggestion of General Woodford, I wrote a letter to Mr. Byington, who was a delegate to several of the early conventions. That gentleman's ill-health prevented his replying, but his nephew stated that Mr. Byington had spoken to him about my letter; that he could not recall any details as to the method of his election as a

necticut. Horace Greeley, who had broken with Seward and Weed in New York and could not possibly be elected from that State and who was "bound to go some how," went as a delegate-at-large to the convention from Oregon.[1]

At 12.10 P. M., Wednesday, May 16th, 1860, the delegates having assembled pursuant to the call set forth below, the convention was called to order by the Hon. Edwin D. Morgan of New York, chairman of the national committee, following the practice of the convention of 1856.

The opening address was made by Mr. Morgan, who nominated for temporary president David Wilmot of Pennsylvania (the author of the Wilmot Proviso) and he was duly chosen.

In calling the convention to order Mr. Morgan said in part:

On the 22nd of December last the Republican National Committee, at a meeting convened for the purpose in the

delegate to the early conventions, but that he remembered attending the Chicago convention and that he spent $200 there which was considered a fabulous extravagance in those days.

[1] Horace Greeley sat at the head of the Oregon delegation. That new State just admitted into the Union was so far from civilization at this time when the iron horse had not yet been heard in either the Rockies or the Sierra Nevada, that the Republican convention selected a number of prominent members in the East including Greeley to represent the State." A. K. McClure, *Our Presidents and How We Make Them,* 158.

"The fact that Greeley represented Oregon was considered a remarkable thing and was much talked about." (The late Mr. Cephas Brainerd in an interview with the writer.)

City of New York, issued a call[1] for a National Convention, which I[2] will now read:

A National Republican Convention will meet at Chicago on Wednesday, the 16th day of May next, at 12 o'clock noon, for the nomination of candidates to be supported for President and Vice-President at the next election.

The Republican electors of the several states, the members of the People's Party of Pennsylvania, and of the Opposition Party of New Jersey, and all others who are willing to co-operate with them in support of the candidates which shall there be nominated, and who are opposed to the policy of the present administration, to federal corruption and usurpation, to the extension of slavery into the territories, to the new and dangerous political doctrine that the Constitution of its own force carries slavery into all the territories of the United States, to the reopening of the African slave trade, to any inequality of rights among citizens and who are in favor of the immediate admission of Kansas into the Union under the constitution recently adopted by its people, of restoring the Federal administration to a system of rigid economy and to the principles of Washington and Jefferson, of maintaining inviolate the rights of the states and defending the soil of every state and territory from lawless invasion, and of preserving the integrity of this Union and the supremacy of the Constitution and laws passed in pursuance thereof against the conspiracy of the leaders of a sectional party to resist the majority principle as established in this government, even at the expense of its existence,—are in-

---

[1] For the details of the proceedings I have referred to *Proceedings of the First Three Republican National Conventions; Conventions of 1856, 1860 and 1864*, republished under the direction of the Republican National Convention of 1892 by Charles W. Johnson, who was secretary of that Convention.

[2] In later conventions this was done by the secretary.

vited to send from each State two delegates from each Congressional district, and four delegates at large to the Convention.

EDWIN D. MORGAN, N. Y., Chairman.	ZACHARIAH CHANDLER, Mich.
	JOHN H. TWEEDY, Wis.
JOSEPH BARTLETT, Me.	ALEX. H. RAMSEY, Minn.
GEORGE G. FOGG, N. H.	ANDREW J. STEVENS, Ia.
LAWRENCE BRAINERD, Vt.	ASA S. JONES, Mo.
JOHN Z. GOODRICH, Mass.	THOMAS WILLIAMS, Penn.
GIDEON WELLES, Conn.	ALFRED CALDWELL, Va.
GEORGE H. HARRIS, Md.	CASSIUS M. CLAY, Ky.
THOMAS SPOONER, Ohio.	MARTIN F. CONWAY, Kas.
JAMES RITCHIE, Ind.	LEWIS CLEPHANE, D. C.
NORMAN B. JUDD, Ill.	CORNELIUS COLE, Cal.
O. P. SCHOOLFIELD, Tenn.	WM. M. CHACE, R. I.
JAMES SHERMAN, N. J.	E. D. WILLIAMS, Del.

Mr. Wilmot, the temporary president having addressed the meeting, it was then moved and carried that a committee consisting of one delegate from each State and Territory represented at this convention be elected by the delegates thereof, who should "report officers to this convention for a permanent organization."

A departure from the practice followed in 1856 of having a joint committee on credentials, rules and appointments was made, at the suggestion of the national committee, and it was agreed that a committee, "consisting of one delegate from each State and Territory represented in the Convention selected by the delgates thereof, be appointed" who should act as a committee on credentials.

Mr. Noble of Iowa then offered a resolution which was adopted "that there be one delegate from each delegation selected by the delegates themselves to act as a committee to prepare the order of business for this Convention."

It was also moved and carried that the rules of the House of Representatives be adopted for the government of the convention until otherwise ordered.

A motion was then made and carried that the roll of the States be called, and that the delegates of each State through their member on the committee present the credentials of that State to the chairman of the committee on credentials.

An adjournment was thereupon taken until five o'clock in the afternoon, when the committee on permanent organization reported George Ashmun [1] of Massachusetts as permanent president of the convention, with a vice-president and secretary from each State and Territory [2] of the Union represented. The report was adopted and an address by Mr. Ashmun then followed. At its conclusion a resolution was moved and adopted that "a committee of one from each State and Territory be appointed to be nominated by the delegates of the respective States on resolutions and platform" and it was also agreed that "all the resolutions submitted to this Convention be referred to that committee without debate."

The chair then called the roll of States and Territories for the purpose of receiving the names of members to constitute a committee on resolutions, and one from each State and Territory was appointed from

[1] The friend of Webster who had labored for his nomination in 1852.

[2] There were 27 vice-presidents and 26 secretaries. For some reason the District of Columbia was not included in the list of secretaries.

each delegation. This finished the work of the first day.

It was then resolved that "the delegations from each State and Territory represented in the convention be requested to designate and report the name of one individual to serve as a member" of the national committee for the ensuing four years.

Mr. Nourse of Iowa moved to amend the resolution so that the delegation should be authorized to select as members of the national committee persons who were not members of the convention. This resolution which was adopted was a change, it will be recalled, from the practice followed in the convention of 1856 but has been the established custom ever since.

The next day the president announced that the reports of the committees were in order.

The committee on order of business and rules made a report which was amended [1] and adopted in the following form:

Rule 1. Upon all subjects before the Convention the States and Territories shall be called in the following order: Maine, New Hampshire, Vermont, Massachusetts, Rhode Island, Connecticut, New York, New Jersey, Pennsylvania, Maryland, Delaware, Virginia, Kentucky, Ohio, Indiana, Missouri, Texas ,Wisconsin, Iowa, California, Minnesota, Oregon, Kansas, Nebraska, District of Columbia.

Rule 2. Four votes shall be cast by the delegates-at-large of each State and each Congressional District shall be entitled to two votes. The votes of each delegation shall be reported by its Chairman, *Provided*, that no delegation shall cast a greater number of votes than there are delegates in

---

[1] For a discussion of this see *infra,* pages 149, 150.

attendance and *Provided,* that this rule shall not conflict with any rule reported by the Committee on Credentials and adopted by the Convention.[1]

Rule 3. The report of the Committee on Platform and Resolutions shall be acted upon before the Convention proceeds to ballot for President and Vice-President.

Rule 4. That a majority of the whole number of votes represented in this Convention according to the votes prescribed by the second rule, shall be required to nominate candidates for President and Vice-President.

Rule 5. The rules of the House of Representatives shall continue to be the rules of this Convention, in so far as they are applicable and not inconsistent with the foregoing rules.

An interesting debate arose on a proposition to require a vote equal to a majority of full delegations from all the States to nominate candidates for President and Vice-President, which, with the delegates actually in attendance, would have been about equivalent to a two-thirds rule,[2] such as is the established rule of procedure in Democratic conventions. This proposition was voted down and the convention de-

---

[1] These latter provisions were necessitated because the report of the committee on credentials which prescribed the basis of representation in the convention appeared to conflict with Rule 2. In the case of Texas and certain other States the committee on credentials had provided that these States should have less votes than would have been accorded to them under this rule and as the report of the committee on credentials had already been adopted, the convention could not very properly adopt a rule which would be inconsistent with this report (*Official Proceedings of the Republican National Convention of 1860,* pp. 124-5-6).

[2] For a fuller discussion of the debate and of the two-thirds rule in Republican national conventions, see *infra,* page 148, *et seq.*

cided by a vote of 358½ to 94½, that only a majority of those present and voting should be required to nominate candidates, and this has been the rule of all subsequent Republican conventions.

The committee on credentials reported the names and numbers of delegates elected from the several States and the votes to which each State was entitled as well as the names of the delegates present and elected from the District of Columbia and the Territories of Kansas and Nebraska, leaving it for the convention to decide whether they should be permitted to vote as members of that body.[1]   Though not named in the call, the Territories of Kansas and Nebraska were each given six votes in the convention.[2]

Next followed the report of the committee on resolutions and platform. The eager convention might have accepted a weak and defective platform, but the committee on the contrary reported one framed with remarkable skill and care. The aim of the committee had been to allow the greatest liberty of sentiment consistent with an emphatic assertion of the cardinal Republican doctrine.   In this they succeeded admirably.[3]

[1] The committee originally reported 8 delegates for Texas.

This led to a serious discussion on the question of apportionment of delegates (see *infra,* page 107) and resulted in recommitting the report which the committee then altered giving Texas but 6 votes. (See also footnote to page 70, *supra.*)

[2] See *supra,* page 41, cf. with 1856.

[3] The full text of the platform may be found in Curtis, *The Republican party,* I, 355, and also in Charles W. Johnson, *Official Report of the Proceedings of the Republican National Convention of 1860,* republished by order of the Convention of 1892, of which he was the secretary.

To recapitulate the chief points of the platform:[1] it denounced disunion, Lecomptonism, the property theory, the dogma that the Constitution carries slavery into the Territories, the re-opening of the slave trade, the popular sovereignty and non-intervention notions and denied "the authority of Congress, of a Territorial legislature, or of individual, to give legal existence to slavery in any Territory of the United States." It opposed any change in the naturalization laws. It recommended an adjustment of import duties to encourage the industrial interests of the whole country. It advocated the immediate admission of Kansas, free homesteads to actual settlers, river and harbor improvements of a national character and a railroad to the Pacific Ocean. Bold on points of common agreement, the convention was unusually successful in avoiding topics of controversy among its supporters or offering grounds of criticism to its enemies. The silence on the "Fugitive Slave Law," on "Personal Liberty Bills," and on the abolition of slavery in the District of Columbia also the avoidance of the direct mention of the Dred Scott decision were significant.[2]

After the vote had been taken on the adoption of the platform, by calling the roll of States[3] and Territories "the delegates and the whole vast audience rose to their feet in a transport of enthusiasm   *   *   *

[1] See Horace Greeley, New York *Tribune,* May 22nd, 1860. Greeley was one of the committee on resolutions. Rhodes, *History of the United States,* II, 464.

[2] Rhodes, *History of the United States,* II, 464.

[3] See Rule 1, *ante,* page 69.

while for many minutes the tremendous cheers and shouts of applause continued."[1]

The convention then adjourned until ten o'clock the next morning.

On the third day, the convention re-assembled pursuant to adjournment. After the delegates had seated themselves, the proceedings were opened by prayer. The chair announced that the business in order was the balloting for a candidate for President of the United States. The convention voted to proceed to a ballot and the chairman stated that it was in order to present names for nomination.

It was a curious feature, in the light of the present day practice, that no pompous nominating speeches were made, like those which formed dramatic features of later conventions,[2] the names being merely formally presented. The following extracts from the *Official Proceedings of 1860* [3] show in a most interesting manner a marked contrast to the unnecessary rhetoric, "electrifying preludes" and long-winded orations which to-day are part of the ceremony in our national conventions.

Mr. Evarts of New York, In the order of business before the Convention, Sir, I take the liberty to name as a candidate to be nominated by this Convention for the office of President of the United States, William H. Seward. (Prolonged applause.)

Mr. Judd of Illinois, I desire on behalf on the delegation from Illinois, to put in nomination as a candidate for

[1] See *Official Proceedings,* etc., p. 142.

[2] Viz.: Robert G. Ingersoll's speech nominating Blaine at Cincinnati in 1876 and Roscoe Conkling's nominating Grant at Chicago, in 1880.

[3] Pages 148 and 149.

President of the United States, Abraham Lincoln of Illinois. (Immense applause, long continued.)

Mr. Dudley of New Jersey, Mr. President, New Jersey presents the name of William L. Dayton.   (Applause.)

Mr. Reader of Pennsylvania, Pennsylvania nominates as her candidate for the Presidency, General Simon Cameron. (Cheers.)

Mr. Cartter of Ohio, Ohio presents to the consideration of this Convention, as a candidate for President, the name of Salmon P. Chase.   (Applause.)

Mr. C. B. Smith of Indiana, I desire, on behalf of the delegation from Indiana, to second the nomination of Abraham Lincoln of Illinois.   (Tremendous applause.)

Mr. Blair of Missouri, I am commissioned by the representatives of the State of Missouri to present to this convention the name of Edward Bates as a candidate for the Presidency.   (Applause.)

Mr. Blair of Michigan, In behalf of the delegates from Michigan, I second the nomination for President of the United States of William H. Seward.   (Loud Applause.)

Mr. Corwin of Ohio, I arise, Mr. President, at the request of many gentlemen, part of them members of this convention, and many of them of [sic] the most respectable gentlemen known to the history of this country and its policies, to present the name of John McLean.   (Applause.)

Mr. Schurz of Wisconsin, I am commissioned by the delegation from the State of Wisconsin to second the nomination of William H. Seward of New York. (Warm applause.)

Various other delegates seconded the several nominees and finally Mr. Andrew of Massachusetts, moved that they "proceed to vote."

The convention then balloted, the States being called in geographical order. At the conclusion of the first ballot, which occupied considerable time, the result was announced by the secretary of the convention as follows:

For William H. Seward of New York, 173½; for Abraham Lincoln of Illinois, 102; for Edward Bates of Missouri, 48; for Simon Cameron of Pennsylvania, 50½; for John McLean of Ohio, 12; for Salmon P. Chase of Ohio, 49; for Benjamin F. Wade of Ohio, 3; for William L. Dayton of New Jersey, 14; for John M. Read of Pennsylvania, 1; for Jacob Collamer of Vermont, 10; for Charles Sumner of Massachusetts, 1; for John C. Fremont of California, 1. The whole number of votes cast, 465; necessary to a choice 233.

The chair stated that no candidate having received a majority of the whole number of votes cast, the convention would proceed to a second ballot.

On the second ballot Seward had 184½, Lincoln 181 and all the rest 99½. To win the Indiana delegation, David Davis, the manager for Lincoln, promised a cabinet position to Caleb Smith, one of the Indiana delegates-at-large, in case of Lincoln's election.[1] To win the support of the close followers of Cameron of Pennsylvania, Davis promised that he too should have "a cabinet position in the event of Lincoln's election and this in addition to the other influences that had been used, secured nearly the whole vote of Pennsylvania."[2] Lincoln himself was ignorant of these bar-

[1] Julian, *Political Recollections,* 182; Herndon, 471.

[2] Herndon, *Lincoln,* III, 471; Lamon, *Life of Abraham Lincoln,* p. 449. Article of A. K. McClure, New York *Sun,* Dec. 13, 1891. See also Julian, *Political Recollections,* p. 182; Curtis, II, 467.

gains at the time and they were made against his positive direction.[1]

On the third ballot Seward had 180, while Lincoln had 231½, lacking but 1½ votes of the necessary number to nominate. Before another ballot could be taken, the change of four votes of Ohio from Chase to Lincoln gave him the nomination. Various other States also changed their votes and the final vote as announced by the secretary was as follows: Whole number of votes cast, 466, necessary to a choice, 234; for Abraham Lincoln of Illinois, 364 votes. The chairman then announced: "Abraham Lincoln of Illinois is selected as your candidate for President of the United States."

Mr. Evarts, the chairman of the New York delegation, moved that the nomination be made unanimous; Mr. Andrews, chairman of the Massachusetts delegation, Mr. Schurz for the delegation of Wisconsin and Mr. Blair for Michigan seconded the motion. This motion was carried amid tumultuous cheering, although no record of a formal vote appears in the official proceedings.[2]

The fact that Mr. Evarts moved that Lincoln's nom-

---

[1] "The responsible position assigned to me comes without conditions." Lincoln to Giddings, May 21st, 1860. Julian, *Life of Giddings,* p. 376.

[2] "The nomination of Lincoln was received in the wigwam with such shouts, cheers and thunders of applause that the report of the cannon on the roof of the building signalling the event could at times hardly be heard inside. The excited masses in the street about the wigwam cried out with delight. Chicago was wild with joy. One hundred guns were fired from the top of the Tremont House. Processions of 'Old Abe' men bearing rails were everywhere to be seen and they celebrated their victory by deep potations of their native beverage." (Rhodes, *History of the United States,* II, 471.)

ination be made unanimous is significant as illustrating the complete party discipline which at this early date prevailed in the Republican ranks, for it was the New York delegation, of which Mr. Evarts was chairman, which had most violently opposed Lincoln's nomination and had been most ardently in favor of Seward.

After a brief adjournment the convention re-assembled and was called to order by the president at five o'clock. The chair announced that the first business in order was to proceed to ballot for a candidate to be supported by the party as its nominee for Vice-President of the United States. Several delegates arose and made nominations. There were cast 466 votes; 234 being necessary for a choice. Hannibal Hamlin of Maine received 357 votes on the second ballot and was nominated as candidate of the Republican party for Vice-President. The motion to make the nomination of Mr. Hamlin unanimous was then put to a vote and carried with enthusiasm. The procedure for the nomination of a candidate for Vice-President was identical with that employed to select the presidential nominee.

On motion of Mr. Tuck of New Hampshire, the president of the convention and the chairmen of the respective State and Territorial delegations were appointed a committee to notify the candidates of their unanimous nomination by the convention.

Mr. Smith of Indiana then moved that the roll of States be called and that each delegation appoint a member of the national committee for the next four years. The roll was then called and a committee selected, consisting of 26 members in all, one being named by each State and Territory represented in the convention.

A resolution of thanks and appreciation of the convention for the "hospitality, taste, zeal and munificence displayed by the ladies and gentlemen of the City of Chicago," then followed, also the thanks of the convention to the Hon. George Ashmun of Massachusetts for the admirable manner in which he had presided over its deliberations, and to the vice-presidents and secretaries for the able manner in which they had discharged their duties.

Mr. Sargeant of California moved that "the Convention do now adjourn *sine die,* with nine cheers for the Convention and the ticket." The motion prevailed and the convention was by the president declared adjourned *sine die.*

At a meeting held in Chicago May 18th, 1860, the national committee organized as it had done four years previously, choosing Hon. Edwin D. Morgan of New York, chairman, and George G. Fogg of New Hampshire, secretary. Subsequently an executive committe, consisting of seven of its members was chosen by the national committee. This was a new departure, for in 1856, when the first Republican national committee organized,[1] no such executive committee was chosen. It has however become an established custom and frequently the chairman of the national committee is called the chairman of the national executive committee.[2] In recent years, when, under a rule adopted by the convention of 1888, the national committee chooses an executive committee, the members

[1] See *supra,* page 54.

[2] See *Proceedings of the National Union Convention held in Baltimore, Md., June 7th and 8th, 1864.*

of which need not be members of the national committee, it sometimes happens that the chairman of this
latter committee is not the same person as the national
committee chairman.

Unlike, the practice in the succeeding national campaigns, the national committee in 1860 did not actually
become the directing body for the ensuing presidential
contest.   Lincoln had campaign managers of his own.[1]

"Nearly all the educational features of the campaign
of 1856 were repeated; the published debates of Lincoln
and Douglas were read with interest and effect; yet
less reliance was placed on newspapers and campaign
documents than in the previous presidential canvass." [2]
Horace Greeley says: "While the circulation of speeches,
campaign lives, and pamphlet essays has not been remarkably large, the number of meetings and oral addresses in this canvass has been beyond precedent.   We
judge that the number of speeches made during the recent campaign has been quite equal to that of all that
were made in the previous presidential canvasses from
1789 to 1856 inclusive." [3]

A large proportion of the voters understood the
several phases of the great slavery issue, its abstract
morality, its economic influence on society, the in-
trigue of the administration and the Senate to make
Kansas a slave State, the judicial status of slavery as
expounded in the Dred Scott decision, the validity and
the effect of the fugitive slave law, the question of the
balance of political power as involved in the choice between slavery extension and slavery restriction and,

[1] See *supra,* page 75.
[2] Rhodes, II, 484.
[3] New York *Tribune,* November 8th, 1860.

reaching beyond even this, the issue, so clearly presented by Lincoln, whether the States should become
ultimately all slave or all free. "In the whole history of
American politics, the voters of the United States
never pronounced a more deliberate judgment than that
which they recorded upon these grave questions at the
presidential election, in November, 1860.

The younger generation of voters who had been
studying the slavery question since 1852, took a vital
interest in this campaign. They read the political literature with avidity. Filled with enthusiasm they were
glad to enroll themselves in the Wide-awake Order [1]
and make manifest their determination to do all in
their power to avert a continuance" [2] of the rule of
the Slave Power. "The Republican party," said Seward
at Cleveland, October 4th, 1860, "is a party chiefly of
young men. Each successive year brings into its rank
an increasing proportion of the young men of this
country." [3]

The presidential election occurred on November 6th,
1860. In seventeen of the free States,—namely, Maine,
New Hampshire, Massachusetts, Rhode Island, Connecticut, Vermont, New York, Pennsylvania, Ohio, Indiana, Illinois, Michigan Wisconsin, Minnesota, Iowa,
California and Oregon,—all the Lincoln electors were
chosen. In one of the free States (New Jersey) the
choice resulted in four electors for Lincoln and three
for Douglas. This assured Lincoln of the votes of

[1] Nicolay and Hay, II, 284.

[2] Rhodes, II, 483.

[3] Seward's Works, Vol. IV, p. 384. On the importance of young
men, see New York *Tribune*, July 30th, 1860.

180 presidential electors or a majority of 57 in the whole electoral college. The fifteen slave States were divided among the other three candidates, Breckenridge, receiving 72 electoral votes; Douglas 12 and Bell 39. Of the popular vote Lincoln had 1,866,542; Douglas 1,376,957; Breckenridge 849,781; Bell 588,879.[1] A majority of almost a million of the total popular vote was against the Republicans.[2]

While in the crisis brought on by the slavery question the old party lines disappeared, yet their system of organization survived.

The Republicans, who represented the new current in the life of the parties, adopted the machinery of the organization in vogue,—the convention and committee system in all its completeness. It was then in such common use that it commanded acceptance almost like a natural phenomenon and indeed, a party, whose origins were so laborious and which had to contend against such powerful opponents, could only hope to

---

[1] Curtis, *The Republican Party,* I, 365; These figures are different in Rhodes, *History of the United States,* II, 500, 501, as follows: Lincoln, 1,857,610; Douglas, 1,291,574; Breckenridge, 850,087; Bell, 646,124.

[2] In round figures the Presidential vote of the Liberty Free-Soil and Republican parties was as follows: subject to allowance for vote not counted in the first four elections:

1840	Birney	7,100
1844	Birney	62,300
1848	Van Buren ⎫ Gerrit Smith ⎬	300,000
1852	John P. Hale	155,900
1856	Fremont	1,341,000
1860	Lincoln	1,900,000

At the North, however, Lincoln's majority over Douglas, Breckenridge and Bell was 293,769,—Greeley's *American Conflict,* I, p. 328.

win by adopting an organization ready at hand, of the type sanctioned by popular customs.

When the second national convention of the Republican party adjourned, May 18th, 1860, the national organization was substantially complete. By that date they had created precedents that were to live for more than half a century,—the call for the national convention by the national committee, the national convention itself, that unique quadrennial political conclave, with its officers temporary and permanent, its rules of procedure, its four great committees, its platform and nominations, the principle of majority nomination of candidates, the fixed number of delegates and the national committee with its chairman, executive committee and vast powers including that of nominating temporary officers for the convention.

CHAPTER III

DEVELOPMENT OF THE REPUBLICAN NATIONAL NOMINATING MACHINERY FROM 1864 TO 1884

The Call. When the Republican party was formed as a national organization in 1856, "its mechanism was patterned and fashioned after that of the late Whig party."[1] In fact the men, who had resigned from the Whig party or the Douglas Democracy in order to enter its ranks, naturally carried with them into the new fold the practices and customs which they had pursued for years in the ranks of the old party.

It was therefore only natural that, when the chairmen of the Republican State committees of Maine, Vermont, Massachusetts, New York, Pennsylvania, Ohio, Michigan, Indiana and Wisconsin desired to call a preliminary gathering or convention to perfect the national organization of the then infant Republican party, they should have issued a call following the customary form adopted by the anti-Masonic party for its first national convention in 1831 and in the same year by the National Republican or Whig party and at regular intervals thereafter by the various national political organizations to summon the great quadrennial party conclave.

With the growth of party organization, both the

[1] These words were used by General Stewart L. Woodford, in the course of an interview with the writer and are a faithful description by a living actor in the scenes of those days.

manner of issuing the call and its form and provisions
have assumed a regularity and system which were
lacking in earlier times. The call for the first national
convention ever held,—the anti-Masonic convention of
1831,—was in the form of a mere resolution of recommendation adopted by a sort of preliminary conference
of delegates. Down to 1852 the call for a national convention was usually issued either by a congressional
caucus or by a caucus of the party members of some
State legislature. At the Democratic convention in
Baltimore on the 22nd day of May, 1848, a committee
was appointed to serve during the ensuing four years,
whose duty it should be among other things to issue
the call for the national convention which the party
would hold in 1852, and from that date in the case of
an established political party this call has been issued
by a permanent body known as the national committee (to which a subsequent chapter is devoted[1]), the
members of which are chosen at each convention to
serve during the four years ensuing.

When "the self-appointed body," [2] consisting of the
chairmen of the State Republican committees of the
nine States mentioned above, issued the call on January 17th, 1856, for the informal convention to be
held at Pittsburg on February 22nd of that year, it had
before it a perfectly definite model. Though it did not
style itself a national committee, it might have done
so more appropriately than the local Washington Association previously referred to which assumed that
designation. Still it must be borne in mind that

[1] *Infra,* Chapter IV.

[2] See *supra,* page 27.

neither of these bodies was a national committee in the sense in which that term is now employed in political literature.

A "National Executive Committee" was appointed at the Pittsburg gathering which issued a call from Washington on the 29th of March, 1856, for the first national convention of the Republican party to meet in Philadelphia on the 17th of June, 1856. The first call bore only five signatures,—a few others being subsequently appended, but this latter call was signed by twenty-two delegates, one from each State represented at the Pittsburg convention and also the District of Columbia, constituting the national executive committee or what was later called merely the national committee.

Whereas the first call invited "the Republicans of the Union to meet in informal convention" for the purpose of perfecting the national organization, the latter call invited the people of the United States to send a certain number of delegates from each State for the purpose of recommending candidates to be supported by the party for the offices of President and Vice-President. In addition to specifying the purposes for which the convention was called and the number of delegates to be sent by each State, the call also fixed the date and place for holding the first national convention of the Republican party.

The call for the convention of 1860 varied but slightly, as we have seen, from that of 1856. It bore the signatures of the members of the national committee chosen at the preceding convention, and named the time and place for holding the next national Republican convention, but differed in this material respect from the call of the Philadelphia convention of 1856, that instead of "three delegates from each congressional district and six delegates at large," each State was invited to send "two delegates from each congressional district and four delegates at large to the convention."

It also differed in this respect that, whereas the previous call had been directed to "the people of the United States without regard to past political differences or divisions" who favored certain principles and were opposed to certain others, this call (the national committee having in the interim been informed as to the temper of the people in the several States) was directed to "the Republican electors of the several States, the members of the People's Party of Pennsylvania and the Opposition Party of New Jersey and all others who are willing to co-operate with them." This call is also significant in that the national committee, which formulated it, presented therein in much detail what they regarded as the precise issues of the hour, such as the right of Congress to prohibit the extension of slavery in the Territories and the immediate admission of Kansas as a free State.

In 1864 certain radical opponents of Mr. Lincoln, forestalled the regular Republican convention by a convention which was held on the 31st day of May at Cleveland,[1] pursuant to a call signed by B. Gratz Brown and others, but we need not concern ourselves with this, which was not a regular party movement and which afterwards withdrew its nominees.

The call for the regular Republican convention was

[1] Curtis, *The Republican Party*, I, 431.

issued from Washington, February 22nd, 1864, although the word "Republican" was avoided, as will be seen from the following [1]:

UNION NATIONAL CONVENTION.

The undersigned who by original appointment, or subsequent designation to fill vacancies, constitute the Executive Committee created by the National Convention held at Chicago on the 16th day of May, 1860, do hereby call upon all qualified voters who desire the unconditional maintenance of the Union, the supremacy of the Constitution and the complete suppression of the existing rebellion with the cause thereof by vigorous war and all apt and efficient means, to send delegates to a convention to assemble at Baltimore on Tuesday, the 7th day of June, 1864, at 12 o'clock noon, for the purpose of presenting candidates for the offices of President and Vice-President of the United States. Each State having a representation in Congress, will be entitled to as many delegates as shall be equal to twice the number of electors to which such State is entitled in the electoral college of the United States.

EDWIN D. MORGAN, N. Y., Chairman,	JOS. GERHARDT, D. of C.
	GIDEON WELLES, Conn.
CHARLES J. GILMAN, Maine.	DENNING DUER, N. J.
E. H. ROLLINS, N. H.	EDWARD McPHERSON, Penn.
L. BRAINERD, Vermont.	N. B. SMITHERS, Delaware.
J. Z. GOODRICH, Mass.	J. F. WAGNER, Maryland.
THOMAS G. TURNER, R. I.	THOMAS SPOONER, Ohio.
H. S. LANE, Indiana.	CARL SCHURZ, Wisconsin.
SAMUEL L. CASEY, Kentucky.	W. D. WASHBURN, Minn.
E. PECK, Illinois.	CORNELIUS COLE, California.

[1] *Proceedings of the First Three Republican National Conventions of 1856, 1860 and 1864,* republished by order of the convention of 1892 by Charles W. Johnson, Secretary (Minneapolis, Minn.).

HERBERT M. HOXIE, Iowa.   WILLIAM A. PHILLIPS, Kan.
AUSTIN BLAIR, Michigan.   O. H. IRISH, Nebraska.
  Washington, February 22, 1864.

The Republican party of 1860 now called itself the "Union Party," and the Republican national committee appointed by the convention which had nominated Lincoln, now called itself, in 1864, the "Union National Committee." The cause is not difficult to ascertain. The war had served to efface in a measure the usual party lines. The Republicans had been compelled to rally to their support all, who believed in a strong union policy, regardless of their previous political affiliations and thus there were found, within the ranks of the so-called Republican party, "disgruntled Whigs, Free-Soilers, and Unionist Democrats whose sole bond of connection was the common opposition to secession" and general support of the first Lincoln administration.

Thus, in 1864, the call for the Republican national convention was worded, as the calls for many of the State conventions had been, so as to include in the invitation everyone regardless of former party relations who would stand by the administration and its measures. It was addressed to all qualified voters "who desire the unconditional maintenance of the Union, the supremacy of the Constitution and the complete suppression of the existing rebellion with the cause thereof by vigorous war and all apt and efficient means." [1] Accordingly, to maintain its appeal to the many different elements it assumed the name of "Union." Even in the campaign of 1868,

[1] See *supra.*

the party used the title "Republican-Union." It was not until the next presidential election in 1872 that the original title "Republican" was definitely assumed;[1] and even then the title "Republican-Union" was used in the calls of 1872 and 1876.

The committee that issued the call in 1864 "took upon themselves the responsibility of suppressing the party name. They describe themselves as 'The undersigned who by original appointment or by subsequent designation to fill vacancies, constitute the Executive Committee created by the National Convention held at Chicago on May 16th, 1860.' " With the exception of the call for the convention of 1880 this call is the briefest ever promulgated by a Republican national committee.[2]

It was on account of the Union Democrats in the convention that Andrew Johnson though a Southern man and a Democrat was placed on the ticket as Vice-President. This nomination and the resultant conflict between the Executive and the Houses of Congress, when Johnson became President, produced a great change in party organization and party leadership by the formation of the so-called congressional committee or congressional campaign committee, a discussion of which is reserved to a subsequent chapter.[3]

In the early conventions of the other parties it had

----

[1] On the reconstruction of the Republican party during the Civil War see William A. Dunning in *American Historical Review*, XVI, 56-63.

[2] See *infra* the call for the convention of 1880.

[3] See *infra*, Chapter IV.

been the general rule to give to each State as many votes as it had electoral votes, while the number of delegates which a State might send was not always fixed. After 1853, however, the number of delegates to the Democratic national convention was definitely fixed at double the number of votes to which the State was entitled in the electoral college,[1] and each delegate was entitled to half a vote in the convention. This was continued by the Democrats until 1872, when the present rule was adopted of allowing to each State twice as many votes as it had votes in the electoral college. The latter method, *i. e.,* twice as many delegates (each entitled to one vote), as a State has votes in its electoral college, has been in vogue in Republican conventions ever since 1860.

As we have seen, the call for the convention of 1856 invited each State to send "three delegates from each congressional district and six delegates at large"; in 1860 "two delegates from each congressional district and four delegates at large." The call for the convention of 1864 declared each State, having a representation in Congress, "entitled to as many delegates as shall be equal to twice the number of electors to which such State is entitled in the electoral college of the United States." This was the same in mathematical

---

[1] Candidates for presidential electors are nominated at State conventions of the respective parties, held either before or after the meeting of the national convention. One elector is nominated for each congressional district in the State and two for the State-at-large. Though usually nominated by the State convention they are sometimes chosen at separate district conventions, or the delegates from the district to the State convention may choose the district elector.

result as the call of 1860,[1] only the States were no longer restricted by the wording of the call as to whether the delegates should represent districts or the State at large. In 1868, as we shall see, still a different form of wording was used, resulting however in the same number of delegates from each State.

Though many Territories and the District of Columbia were represented in the conventions of 1860 and 1864, nothing was said as yet in the calls for these respective conventions regarding the sending of delegates by any Territory or the District of Columbia. This, we shall see, was provided for as to the Territories for the first time in the call for the convention of 1872 and as to the District of Columbia, in the call for the convention of 1876.

On Wednesday, May 20th, 1868, a call [2] was issued for the National Union Republican convention to be held at Chicago, May 20th of that year as follows:

NATIONAL UNION REPUBLICAN CONVENTION.

The undersigned, constituting the National Committee designated by the Convention held at Baltimore on the 7th of June, 1864, do appoint that a Convention of the Union Republican party be held in the City of Chicago, on Wednesday the 20th day of May next, at 12 o'clock M. for the purpose of nominating candidates for the offices of President and Vice-President of the United States.

Each State in the United States is authorized to be represented in said Convention by a number of delegates equal

---

[1] See *supra.*

[2] *Official Proceedings of the National Union Republican Convention, held at Chicago May 20th and 21st, 1868,* reported by Ely, Burnham and Bartlett, Official Reporters of the convention, Chicago, 1868.

to twice the number of Senators and Representatives, to which each State is entitled in the National Congress.

We invite the co-operation of all citizens who rejoice that our great Civil War has happily terminated in the discomforture of rebellion, who would hold fast the unity and integrity of the Republic, and maintain its paramount right to defend to the utmost its existence, whether imperilled by a secret conspiracy or armed force: [sic] of an economical administration of the public expenditures; of the complete extirpation of the principles and policy of slavery and of the speedy reorganization of those States whose governments were destroyed by the rebellion, and the permanent restoration to their proper practical relations with the United States, in accordance with the true principles of a republican government.

MARCUS L. WARD, N. J.	JOHN D. DE FREES, Ind.,
Chairman.	*Secretary.*
S. J. BOWEN, D. C.	J. B. CLARK, N. J.
WM. CLAFLIN, Mass.	A. B. GARDNER, Vt.
J. S. FOWLER, Tenn.	S. A. PURVIANCE, Penn.
MARSH GIDDINGS, Mich.	B. C. COOK, Ill.
A. W. CAMPBELL, W. Va.	D. B. STUBBS, Ia.
N. B. SMITHERS, Del.	H. C. HOFFMAN, Md.
W. A. PILE, Mo.	W. J. COWING, Va.
S. JUDD, Wis.	C. L. ROBINSON, Fla.
H. H. STARKWEATHER, Conn.	HORACE GREELEY, N. Y.
WM. WINDOM, Minn.	B. R. COWEN, Ohio.
D. R. GOODLOE, N. C.	N. EDMUNDS, Dak.
SAMUEL CRAWFORD, Kan.	THOS. G. TURNER, R. I.
J. P. CHAFFEE, Col.	S. F. HERSEY, Me.

It should be noticed that the phraseology used to designate the number of delegates to which each State was entitled, though differing from that previously employed, produced exactly the same mathematical result and, as we shall see, has been employed almost constantly in succeeding calls for Republican national conventions; but, no matter what the language, the representation of the State in the convention has always equalled twice its representation in the electoral college of the United States.

Here again we note a change of party names. The Republican party of 1856 and 1860 and the Union party of 1864 now, in the call of 1868, emerged as the National Union Republican party,[1]—the name being a sort of combination of its earlier appellations.

The calls, as the reader may have noticed, have with one exception been growing longer and more elaborate with each year. Hitherto they contained only designs for the future, but in 1872 the call [2] for the fifth quadrennial convention of the Republican party contained an elaborate description of the party's past performances, as will be seen from the following:

The undersigned, constituting the National Committee designated by the Convention held at Chicago on the 20th of May, 1868, hereby call a Convention of the Union Republican Party at the City of Philadelphia, on Wednesday, the 5th day of June next, at 12 o'clock noon, for the purpose of nominating candidates for the offices of President and Vice-President of the United States.

Each State is authorized to be represented in the convention by delegates equal to twice the number of Senators and Representatives to which it will be entitled in the next National Congress, and each organized Territory is authorized to send two delegates.

[1] See *Official Proceedings, etc., 1868*.

[2] Curtis, *The Republican Party*, II, 11; *Proceedings of the National Union Republican Convention held at Philadelphia, June 5 and 6, 1872*, reported by Francis H. Smith, officially reported and printed by Gibson Bros., Printers, Washington, 1872.

In calling this Convention, the Committee remind the country that the promises of the Union Republican Convention of 1868 have been fulfilled. The States lately in rebellion have been restored to their former relations to the government. The laws of the country have been faithfully executed, public faith has been preserved, and the national credit firmly established. Governmental economy has been illustrated by the reduction, at the same time, of the public debt and of taxation; and the funding of the national debt at a lower rate of interest has been successfully inaugurated. The rights of naturalized citizens have been protected by treaties, and immigration encouraged by liberal provisions. The defendants of the Union have been gratefully remembered, and the rights and interests of labor recognized. Laws have been enacted, and are being enforced, for the protection of persons and property in all sections. Equal suffrage has been engrafted on the National Constitution; the privileges and immunities of American citizenship have become a part of the organic law and a liberal policy has been adopted toward all who engaged in the rebellion. Complications in foreign relations have been adjusted in the interests of peace throughout the world, while the national honor has been maintained. Corruption has been exposed, offenders punished, responsibility enforced, safeguards established, and now, as heretofore, the Republican Party stands pledged to correct all abuses and carry out all reforms necessary, to maintain the purity and efficiency of the public service. To continue and firmly establish its fundamental principles, we invite the co-operation of all the citizens of the United States.

WILLIAM CLAFLIN, Mass., *Chairman.*	WM. E. CHANDLER, N. H., *Secretary.*
JOHN A. PETERS, Me.	THOS. W. OSBORN, Fla.
LUKE P. POLAND, Vt.	L. C. CARPENTER, S. C.

L. B. Frieze, R. I.
H. H. Starkweather, Conn.
James Gopsill, N. J.
W. K. Kemble, Pa.
H. M. Jenkins, Del.
B. R. Cowen, Ohio.
John Coburn, Ind.
C. B. Farwell, Ill.
Zachariah Chandler, Mich.
J. T. Averill, Minn.
David Atwood, Wisc.
G. W. McCrary, Iowa.
C. C. Fulton, Md.
F. Stearns, Va.
John R. Hubbard, W. Va.
Wm. Sloan, N. C.

J. H. Caldwell, Ga.
J. P. Stow, Ala.
M. H. Southworth, La.
A. C. Fisk, Miss.
S. C. Pomeroy, Kan.
B. F. Rice, Ark.
J. B. Clark, Mo.
A. B. Burton, Ky.
H. Maynard, Tenn.
E. B. Taylor, Neb.
J. W. Nye, Nev.
H. W. Corbett, Ore.
G. C. Gorham, Cal.
J. V. Chaffee, Colo.
W. A. Burleigh, Dak.
Sayles J. Bowen, D. of C.

Washington, D. C., Jan. 11th, 1872.

This was the first call which provided expressly for territorial representatives. They had previously attended the conventions but the call had never heretofore recognized them; from now on it always did. As to the number of delegates, the rule followed is exactly that of the call for the preceding convention.

The call [1] for the convention of 1876, of which the following is a copy, is significant in that the name "Union Republican National Convention" was still continued and in addition to territorial representa-

[1] Curtis, *The Republican Party*, II, 47; *Proceedings of the Republican National Convention, held at Cincinnati, Ohio, June 14, 15 and 16, 1876, resulting in the nomination for President and Vice-President of Rutherford P. Hayes and William A. Wheeler,* officially reported by M. A. Clancey, of Washington, D. C. Printed by Republican Press Association in Concord, New Hampshire, 1876.

tion in the convention, express provision was made for representation of the District of Columbia which, like each of the Territories was given two delegates:

The next Union Republican National Convention, for the nomination of candidates for President and Vice-President of the United States, will be held in the city of Cincinnati, on Wednesday, the fourteenth day of June, 1876, at 12 o'clock noon, and will consist of delegates from each State equal to twice the number of its senators and representatives in Congress, and of two delegates from each organized Territory and the District of Columbia.

In calling the conventions for the election of delegates, the committees of the several States are recommended to invite all Republican electors, and all other voters, without regard to past political differences or previous party affiliations, who are opposed to reviving sectional issues, and desire to promote friendly feeling and permanent harmony throughout the country by maintaining and enforcing all the constitutional rights of every citizen, including the full and free exercise of the right of suffrage without intimidation and without fraud; who are in favor of the continued prosecution and punishment of all official dishonesty, and of an economical administration of the government by honest, faithful, and capable officers; who are in favor of making such reforms in government as experience may from time to time suggest; who are opposed to impairing the credit of the nation by depreciating any of its obligations, and in favor of sustaining in every way the national faith and financial honor; who hold that the common-school system is the nursery of American liberty, and should be maintained absolutely free from sectarian control; who believe that, for the promotion of these ends, the direction of the government should continue to be confided to those who adhere to the principles of 1776, and support them as incorporated in the constitution and the laws; and who are in favor of recognizing and strength-

ening the fundamental principle of national unity in this
centennial anniversary of the birth of the republic.

E. D. MORGAN, *Chairman,*

WM. E. CHANDLER, *Secretary,*

Republican National Committee.

Washington, January 13, 1876.

It should also be noted that this call was signed only
by the chairman and secretary of the national committee and did not bear the signatures of all of the
individual members of that committee.

With reference to the number of delegates from
each State the same language was used as in the
several preceding calls and the call also contained an
elaborate expression of the principles of the party.

In the call [1] for the seventh Republican national
convention to meet at Chicago, June 2nd, 1880, of
which the following is a copy, we notice certain
changes:

Washington, January, 1880.

A National Convention of the Republican Party will meet
at Chicago, on Wednesday, the second day of June next, at
twelve o'clock, for the nomination of candidates to be supported for President and Vice-President of the next election.
Republicans and all who will co-operate with them in supporting the nominees of the party, are invited to choose two
delegates from each Congressional district, four at large from
each State, two from each Territory, and two from the District of Columbia, to represent them in the Convention.

J. D. CAMERON, *Chairman,*

THOS. B. KEOGH, *Secretary.*

[1] *Political Manual for 1880,* edited and compiled by Stiles &
Hutchins, 74 *et seq.*

This is the briefest of all the calls. It contains no references to past performances or future party principles. The appeal is made only to "Republicans and all who will co-operate with them in supporting the nominees of the party." "The party was no longer an infant, and the principles it stood for were known; twenty years had elapsed since the federal government was first committed to its charge and the national committee doubtless felt that the brief language above employed was more significant than any elaborate declaration of principles in that place would have been."

The language of the preceding calls with regard to the number of delegates from each State has been changed. Instead of "delegates * * * equal to twice the number of its Senators and Representatives in Congress," which was employed in most of the preceding calls, we find now, "two delegates from each congressional district and four at large from each State," harking back to the language of the call of 1860, but, as has been heretofore mentioned, the result, as far as the number of delegates which each State was entitled to send was concerned, was exactly the same as in previous years and has never varied since the call of 1860, no matter what the change or terminology may have been.

In returning to the language of the call of 1860,[1] a form which has been substantially employed in all

---

[1] "It will thus be seen that the call for 1880, in inviting "two delegates from each Congressional district, four delegates at large from each State," purposely passes to and expressly adopts the language of the earlier calls of 1856 and 1860.

This form of call for this Convention was not, it may fairly be presumed, adopted without a purpose. It was expressly intended to remove any doubt which might possibly be raised and to make positive and indisputable district representation, which had its origin with the

the calls succeeding that of 1876, the national committee defined not only the number of delegates to which each State was entitled, but also indicated that certain delegates were from congressional districts and the others from the State at large.

The custom established in 1876 of having the chairman and the secretary of the national committee sign in lieu of the individual signatures of the members of that committee we find was again followed. This became the settled practice though occasionally (as in 1900) the call for the convention. This call was issued by the executive committee of the national committee and signed by the chairman of that committee, who, by reason of a special provision [1] adopted at a later convention, was not necessarily a member of the real national committee at all.

At the convention of 1880, over 100 pages of the published proceedings of the Republican national convention are devoted to the discussion over contested seats.[2] In order, if possible, to prevent a repetition of such a state of affairs, Mr. Boutwell [3] of Massachusetts introduced an amendment to the report of the committee on rules, which was adopted, to the effect that the national Republican committee should within twelve months "prescribe a method or methods for the

birth of the Republican party as shown by the calls for the Conventions of 1856 and 1860." (Extract from the report of the committee on credentials as presented by its chairman, Mr. O. D. Conger, to the convention of 1880. See *Official Procedings of the Convention of 1880*, p. 422.)

[1] See *infra,* page 207.

[2] *Proceedings of the Republican National Convention, held at Chicago, Illinois, June 2d, 3d, 4th, 5th, 7th and 8th, 1880*, pp. 45-150.

[3] *Ibid,* 126.

election of delegates to the Republican national convention to be held in 1884" and "issue a call for that convention in conformity therewith," provided that nothing in such rules or methods should be so construed as to prevent the several congressional districts in the United States from selecting their own delegates to the national convention.

The national committee held a meeting at Washington in 1883, at which an attempt was made to change the basis of representation at the national convention. No change in this respect was made however and the old basis was readopted; but a change was made in the choice of delegates by limiting the time for the holding of State conventions preceding the national conventions to not less than thirty days before the time of the national convention.[1] This has remained unchanged.

By this means the action of the national convention could not be too easily anticipated by the States and more power was given to the minority.

Previous to 1884, the Republican national committee in calling the convention gave no instructions as to the method of selecting delegates; but the call for that year specified that the four delegates-at-large should be chosen by State conventions and gave to the Republicans in the congressional districts the option of electing delegates by district conventions fifteen days before the State convention, or by district delegates at the meeting of the State convention. [1]

[1] Mr. Curtis has made a slight error in stating that the time was limited to "not less than thirty nor more than sixty days, *vide* Curtis, *The Republican party,* II, 116, and his conclusions there stated are evidently wrong.

The call for 1884 was as follows:

Washington, D. C., Dec. 12, 1883.

A National Republican Convention will meet at Chicago, Ill., Tuesday, June 3d, 1884, at 12 o'clock noon, for the nomination of candidates to be supported for President and Vice-President at the next election.

The Republican electors of the several States, and all other voters, without regard to past political differences, who are in favor of elevating and dignifying American labor, protecting and extending home industries, giving free popular education to the masses of the people, securing free suffrage and an honest counting of ballots, effectually protecting all human rights in every section of our common country; and who desire to promote friendly feeling and permanent harmony throughout the land by maintaining a National government pledged to these objects and principles, are cordially invited to send from each State four delegates-at-large, and from each Congressional district two delegates, and for each representative-at-large two delegates to the Convention.

The delegates-at-large shall be chosen by popular State Conventions, called on not less than twenty days' published notice, and not less than thirty days before the time fixed for the meeting of the National Convention.

The Republicans of the various Congressional districts shall have the option of electing their delegates at separate popular delegate conventions, called on similar notice, and held in the Congressional districts at any time within the fifteen days next prior to the meeting of the State conventions, or by sub-divisions of the State Conventions into District Conventions; and such delegates shall be chosen in the

---

[1] *Official Proceedings of the Republican National Convention, etc., 1884.*

latter method if not elected previous to the meeting of the State Conventions. All district delegates shall be accredited by the officers of such District Conventions.

Two delegates shall be allowed from each Territory and from the District of Columbia, similarly chosen.

Notices of contest shall be given to the National Committee, accompanied by full printed statements of the grounds of contests, which shall be made public; and preference in order of hearing and determining contests shall be given by the Convention according to the dates of the reception of such notices and statements by the National Committee.

D. M. SABIN, Minnesota, *Chairman.*

JOHN A. MARTIN, Kansas, *Secretary.*

The convention of 1884 [1] adopted the rule that 'each Congressional district in the United States shall elect its delegates to the National Convention *in the same way as the nomination for a member of Congress is made in said District.*'[2] With slight modifications this

[1] Dallinger, *Nominations for Elective Office,* 43 is apparently an error when he says 1892.

[2] "The Republican rule gives increased importance to the congressional district and tends to make it a more significant factor in party organization." The Democratic rule, see *infra,* page 104, makes the State the unit and tends to the retention of larger powers in the State conventions. (J. Macy, *Party Organization and Machinery,* 83-84.) "The Republican method assures the people in each congressional district a voice in the proceedings of the convention."

A copy of the official call is sent to the State committee of the party in each State; thereupon the State committee proceeds to call a State convention for the purpose of choosing the four delegates from the State at large, and at the same time notifies the party committees in the different congressional districts of the State. In each congressional district there is usually a congressional district committee, consisting of one or more members from each city and town in the district. These in turn proceed to call the congressional district convention, to choose the two delegates and alter-

rule has been embodied in each call for the convention since that date. An illustration of it is shown in the following call for the convention of 1888.[1]

To the Republican Electors of the United States: In accordance with usage and obedient to the instructions of the Republican National Convention of 1884, a National Convention of delegated representatives of the Republican party will be held at the City of Chicago, Ill., on Tuesday the 19th of June, 1888, at 12 o'clock noon, for the purpose of nominating candidates for President and Vice-President to be supported at the next National election and for the transaction of such other business as may be there presented. Republican electors in the several States, and voters without regard to past political affiliations, differences or action, who believe in the American principle of a protective tariff for the defence and development of home industries, and the elevation of home labor and who would reduce the National taxes and prevent the accumulation of the surplus in the Treasury in harmony with this principle; who are opposed to the attempt now more openly avowed than ever before to establish a policy which would strike down American labor to the level of the underpaid and oppressed workers of foreign lands; who favor a system of naval and coast defences which will enable the United States to conduct its international negotiations with self respect; who gratefully cherish the defenders of our country; who condemn and resent the continued and unjust exclusion of rapidly growing Territories which have an indisputable title to admission into the Sisterhood of States; who are in favor of free schools and popular education—a free and honest

nates from each congressional district. The delegates to both the State and district conventions are chosen at caucuses and primaries in the different cities and towns. (Dallinger, *supra*, p. 76.)

[1] *Official Proceedings of the Republican National Convention, etc.,* *1888.*

ballot, and a fair count; the protection of every citizen of the United States in his legal rights at home and abroad; a foreign policy that shall extend our trade and commerce to every land and clime, and shall properly support the dignity of the Nation, and the promotion of friendly and harmonious relations and intercourse between all the States, are cordially invited to unite under this call in the formation of a National ticket. Each State will be entitled to four delegates-at-large, and for each Representative-at-large two delegates, and each Congressional district, each Territory and the District of Columbia to two delegates. The delegates-at-large shall be chosen by popular State conventions called on not less than twenty days' published notice, and not less than thirty days before the meeting of the National Convention. The Congressional district delegates shall be chosen in the same manner as the nomination of a member of Congress is made in said district. The Territorial delegates shall be chosen in the same manner as the nomination of a Delegate in Congress is made. The delegates from the District of Columbia shall be chosen at a convention constituted of members elected in primary district assemblies held under the call and direction of the Republican Central Committee of said District. An alternate delegate for each delegate in the National Convention, to act in case of the absence of the delegate, shall be elected in the same manner and at the same time as the delegate is elected. In addition to their regular delegates each of the Territories of Dakota and Washington are [sic] authorized by vote of this committee to choose four contingent delegates, the admission of said contingent delegates to be determined by the action of the next Republican National Convention. All notices of contest must be filed with the National Committee in writing, accompanied by printed statements of the grounds of contest, which shall be made public. Preference in the order of hearing and determining contests will be given by the convention in accordance with the dates of filing of such notices and statements with the National Committee.

B. F. JONES, *Chairman.*

SAMUEL FESSENDEN, *Secretary.*

Washington, D. C., Dec. 9, 1887.

Although the convention of 1888 was not to meet until June of that year, the call was issued by the national committee in December 1887 in compliance with a rule adopted at the convention of 1884, that "such committee shall issue the call for the meeting of the National Committee six months at least before the time fixed for said meeting." In 1896, this was changed to sixty days instead of six months and this practice has since prevailed.

In prescribing the methods of electing delegates, the calls of the Democratic and Republican parties differ fundamentally.[1] The Republican party has formulated the rule mentioned above, definitely stipulating that the four delegates-at-large shall be chosen at the State convention and the other delegates at congressional district conventions (special provisions being made for the Territories and for the States that prescribe nomination by direct primaries), but the Democratic national organization has limited its authority in determining its own composition to the mere act of notifying the various States and Territories of the number of delegates which they are entitled to send, leaving to the States the manner of choosing those delegates.[2]

Apportionment of Delegates. In the matter of apportionment of delegates, there is a wide difference in

[1] C. A. Beard, *American Government and Politics,* 167.

[2] J. Macy, *Party Organization and Machinery,* 83.

practice between State and national conventions. In the States, the number of delegates assigned to the different areas is usually based to a greater or less extent upon the party vote for the leading candidates in the last preceding State or national election, but in the national conventions, the rule, as we have seen, adopted by the call of 1860, giving each State a representation on the fixed basis of twice as many delegates as it has Representatives and Senators in Congress, has been followed ever since without change.[1]

It should be noted that according to the fixed rule of representation of the States in the national convention, relative party strength in the different States is not considered at all.

In Republican conventions, the irregularities of the present system of apportionment are especially noticeable. In the South, the Republican party is so weak that in some States there is practically no party organization at all. Nevertheless, under the present system, each of the Southern States sends twice as many delegates to the national convention as it has votes in the electoral college. For example, at the convention of 1892, South Carolina cast the same number of votes and therefore had as much weight in selecting party candidates as Kansas, although, at the preceding presidential election, the Republican candidate received

---

[1] The Republicans adopted this rule of membership in 1860 and it has been the rule of both parties since 1872 (Prof. Macy, Chicago *Record,* Monday, March 13th, 1900).

As to apportionment to congressional districts see *supra,* pages 97 and 98.

only 13,736 votes in the former State as against 182,904 in the latter.[1]

The question of apportionment was discussed as early as the convention of 1860 [2] and resulted in recommitting the report to the committee on credentials and the reduction of the vote of the State of Texas to which we have previously referred.[3]

Though the question had been occasionally raised in subsequent conventions no important attempt to change the basis of representation at the national convention was made until the meeting of the Republican national committee at Washington in 1883 to which we have already alluded and which resulted in a con-

[1] Again in 1904, Mississippi in which there were only 3,168 Republican voters sent 20 delegates to the Republican convention and Michigan with 216,651 Republican voters sent only 22 delegates. This of course helps to prevent each party from becoming sectional in character. It is partially offset by the Democratic rule requiring a two-thirds vote to nominate.

When a Republican President in office is a candidate for renomination, this evil is aggravated by the fact that the delegations from the Southern "pocket boroughs" are made up almost wholly of the federal office holders in those States, who have a personal interest in securing the renomination of the man to whom they owe their positions. The evil, however, can be remedied easily it would seem, by apportioning the number of delegates to some extent at least with reference to the vote cast in the different States for the party candidates at the preceding presidential election, a method already in vogue in both parties in the choice of delegates to State conventions.

[2] "We are a convention of delegates representing a party having constituencies at home. This is not a mass convention * * * but a convention of delegates representing a constituency and having constituents at home to represent. * * * They have never had a Republican party in Maryland. * * * The true policy of the Republican party is to allow its members a voice but in proportion to their numbers." Remarks of David Wilmot; see *Official Proceedings of the Republican Convention of 1856*, pp. 111, *et seq.*

[3] See *supra*, page 70, footnote No. 1.

tinuation of the old practice.

In 1888, the committee on rules, which had been asked to make a report upon the resolution that had been referred to them in regard to the apportionment of delegates to future national conventions, presented a majority and minority report. The minority report, which was an attempt to suggest a method, whereby the number of delegates to future conventions should be more nearly proportionate to the Republican votes cast in the respective States, was rejected and the majority report, was adopted reading as follows:

First:—Each State shall be entitled to four delegates-at-large and to two additional delegates-at-large for each representative-at-large if any, elected in such State at the last preceding Congressional election.

Second:—Each Territory and the District of Columbia shall be entitled to two delegates.

Third:—Each Congressional district shall be entitled to two delegates,

and this has continued to be the rule with the exception of changes in regard to the Territories.[1]

In 1892, the Republican national committee again took up the matter of apportionment of delegates. At a meeting of the committee, held at Washington on June 27th, the member of the national committee from West Virginia offered the following resolution:

"Resolved: That the call for the next national Republican convention be upon the following basis: Two delegates from each State as delegates-at-large; one delegate from each Congressional District in the United States and an additional delegate for each 7000 votes cast in any Republican district at the Presidential election of 1892, and a dele-

[1] See *infra*, page 110.

gate for the fraction of 7000 votes greater than one half and two delegates from each Territory and the District of Columbia.''

There was some doubt whether under the rules the national committee had any authority to make this radical change. Accordingly, a circular letter was sent to the leading members of the party in all parts of the country, to ascertain the general sentiment of the party before definite action was taken by the committee. But the Republican convention of 1896 met and adjourned without any proceeding whatever in regard to this important matter, and, though the subject was debated in subsequent conventions, no action has ever been taken.

Besides the States, Territories (represented in Congress by delegates only without a vote) and the District of Columbia (not represented at all) are empowered to take part in the convention. Their populations are not allowed to vote for the President, but in order to develop party life and party strength in the Territories in anticipation of their coming into the Union as States, the organization of the party concedes to them and also by courtesy to the District of Columbia, to Alaska, Indian Territory, Hawaii, Porto Rico and the Philippine Islands, representation at the national conventions.

The Republican party has always dealt liberally with the Territories, but it was some years, as we have seen, before the call specifically assigned any right to the Territories and to the District of Columbia to send delegates to the national convention. The former received this recognition in 1872 and the latter in 1876.

In the Republican conventions, the territorial delegates vote as other delegates, but in the Democratic
conventions the territorial delegates have no voice.
The number of delegates assigned to the Territories
has usually varied from convention to convention.
Thus in 1856, Kansas, then a Territory, was given nine
votes in the convention. In 1860, Kansas and Nebraska were each given six votes. In 1864 the Territories of Nebraska, Colorado and Nevada were allowed
six votes each but certain Territories and the District
of Columbia (which had been allowed to vote in 1860,
though apparently not in 1856) although their delegations were admitted to the convention with all the
rights and privileges of delegates were denied the right
to vote.[1]   In 1868 and 1876 Colorado was given six
votes.

In recent years, the call has specifically allotted to
each Territory and the District of Columbia a definite
number of delegates,—two in each of the conventions
held in the years 1880, 1884, 1888 and 1892,[2] with the

[1] In 1864 a delegate from New Mexico asked permission to allow
the delegates from New Mexico to record their votes for President,
this being the first time that this Territory had sent delegates to a
Republican convention. Another delegate from New Mexico moved
that the remaining other organized Territories of the United States
which had sent delegates to the convention who had not theretofore been allowed to vote be permitted to record their votes, and it
was also moved to extend this resolution to the District of Columbia,
which had not been permitted to vote at this convention. These
several motions were lost, but the convention carried the resolution
of a New York delegate that the secretaries might receive any communications which these various delegations might see fit to make,
showing their sentiments in favor of the nomination of Lincoln and
Johnson, in order that those communications might go on the minutes.

[2] The rules adopted in the convention allowed New Mexico six
delegates but restricted all the other Territories to two.

authorization in the call of 1888 that Dakota and Washington might each send four more additional delegates, whose admission to the national convention would be contingent upon the action of that body.[1] In 1896 [2] and 1900, the call allotted two delegates with a recommendation in that of 1896 that the Territories of Utah, New Mexico, Oklahoma and Arizona should send four more additional delegates, whose admission to the national convention the committee would recommend, and in 1900 there was a similar recommendation of six additional delegates for the Territories of Arizona, Indian Territory, New Mexico and Oklahoma, and four for Alaska. In 1904 the call prescribed two for the District of Columbia, six for the Territories of Arizona, New Mexico, Oklahoma and Hawaii and Indian Territory, and four for Alaska, but in 1908 the rule of two for the Territories was resumed.

In addition to the regular delegates an "alternate" is appointed for each delegate to take the place of such delegate in case he is prevented from attending the national convention. The alternates are elected at the same time and in the same manner as the delegates; they sit in the convention immediately behind the delegates.

It has been the universal custom, where any of the four delegates-at-large is absent, to permit the alter-

[1] The rules adopted in the convention allowed Dakota ten delegates, Washington, six, but restricted all the other Territories to two.

[2] The rules adopted in the convention allowed six delegates to Arizona, Indian Territory, New Mexico and Oklahoma, four to Alaska and two to the District of Columbia, and similarly succeeding conventions have adopted specific rules irrespective of the call with regard to the number of delegates to which the several Territories were to be entitled in the convention.

nates in their order on the list to take their places, and
where one district delegate is absent, if his alternate be
also absent the second alternate chosen by the same
constituents is permitted to act. In other words, an
alternate may vote in the convention although he may
not be the special alternate of the delegate to whom he
is attached.

The Work of the Convention. The Republican convention meets in the summer of the "Presidential
Year," that is to say, of that year in which the people
will have to choose, on the first Tuesday in November,
the presidential electors, who according to the letter of
the Constitution elect the President and Vice-President.
This has been the custom from the earliest Republican
conventions held, such as the Pittsburg convention of
1856, which met in June of that year, and the convention of 1860, which met in May of that year.

Long before the meeting of the convention, the
friends of the leading aspirants proceed to organize in
each State and endeavor in every way to get as many
State and district conventions as possible to support
their favorites' candidacy at the coming national convention. The newspapers publish the comparative
standing of the various candidates, giving the returns
from each State and district convention as they come
in and revising their estimates, from day to day, until
the election of delegates in all parts of the country
has been completed.

After all the delegates have been chosen, the contest is transferred from the States to the convention
city, selected by the national committee, as more particularly discussed elsewhere herein. The partisans of

each of the leading candidates are already in the field. They open their own particular headquarters, in one of the leading hotels, and endeavor, by means of meetings of delegates, open-air rallies and processions, to arouse all the enthusiasm possible in the interest of their favorite candidate. This practice had been associated with national conventions from the earliest days, although the Whig proceedings are traditionally supposed to have observed a certain amount of dignity and decorum. The first Republican national convention, it is true, lacked much of this, because the contest which was about to follow seemed but a tentative effort in a new and untried cause.[1] At the Republican convention of 1860, however, we find torchlight processions, parades, badges and the usual demonstrations in favor of this or that prospective nominee with which we to-day are so familiar, and since that time they have become regularly identified with conventions and political gatherings generally.

At the delegation headquarters in the various hotels, "deals" between the leaders of the different factions are consummated, votes are traded for promises of patronage or for something more tangible and in short, all the secret "wire-pulling" is carried on which, frequently, beginning with Chicago in 1860,[2] has had such an important effect upon the final action of the convention.

In the very first Republican convention, there was a certain recognition of each "State delegation" with its chairman, as a unit, but, in 1860, this became even more definitely established. Thus the delegation is ex-

[1] See *supra,* page 62.
[2] See *supra,* page 75.

pected to and has, ever since that time, kept together during the convention. It usually travels together to the place of meeting, takes rooms in the same hotel, has recognized headquarters there, sits in a particular place allotted to it in the convention hall, around the banner of its State, and holds meetings of its members during the progress of the convention to decide upon the course which it shall take from time to time, and has a chairman to direct its part in the convention. Some of the more important delegations are accompanied by brass bands and often carry curious symbols and transparencies.

The sittings of the national convention, usually held in an enormous building, sometimes constructed particularly for the purpose, are public and early attracted from ten to fifteen thousand spectators. The convention of 1856 met at Musical Fund Hall in Philadelphia, but, in 1860, it required a wigwam [1] specially fitted and constructed for the occasion to accommodate the thousands which had gathered. In 1864, the Front Street Theatre in Baltimore was employed. In 1868, Crosby's Opera House at Chicago; in 1872, the Academy of Music at Philadelphia, the largest building of the kind in the City, was required to accommodate the gathering; in 1876, the national convention met at Exposition Hall, Chicago, a building which, as its name implies, had been used for exposition purposes and seated about 15,000 persons comfortably. This building was again used in 1880 and in 1884.

---

[1] See *supra,* page 60 and footnote.

The delegates who had increased from 565 in 1856, to 820 in number in 1884 are "a mere drop in the ocean of faces." [1] "In the audience are usually gathered the most active politicians who are not serving as delegates, enthusiastic partisans from all over the country and interested visitors, attracted by the spectacular affair." They are admitted by tickets which are partly sold to cover the expenses of the convention and partly distributed to the delegates, who can give them to their friends. Sometimes the convention passes a special resolution that a certain number of tickets be given to such and such an organization or to the veterans of the Civil war assembled in the convention city.

All the preliminary arrangements for the convention are and have been from earliest times entrusted to the national committee—in later years to a particular branch thereof known as the executive committee of the national committee. A detailed discussion thereof is reserved to a later chapter, suffice it to say here that, beginning with the local Washington committee (which assumed the name of "National Committee"), all of the preliminary arrangements,—electing [2] a sergeant-at-arms for the convention, superintending the printing of tickets, organizing a force to act as assistants, ushers and pages to seat the people and to maintain order during the sessions of the convention,—are taken charge of by the members of the national committee. Prior to the opening of the convention they have

[1] J. Bryce, *American Commonwealth*, II, 192.

[2] The sub-committee of the national committee on the recommendation of the executive and finance committee appoints the sergeant-at-arms.

also arranged many other details of organization, determined upon the general programme of procedure, fixed upon the temporary and permanent chairman and a general list of the other temporary officers, reached a decision upon the greater part of the contested seats from which they have made up a temporary roll of delegates and have determined upon the main features of the party platform,—their decision in the two latter cases being subject of course to the approval of the committees on credentials and resolutions which are subsequently elected by the convention.

The National Republican convention which met in Baltimore December 12th, 1831, and nominated Henry Clay for President, was the general prototype for practice and procedure of the many other conventions, Republican and otherwise, which followed. An examination of its proceedings [1] shows that in the appointment of committees, adoption of rules and course of procedure it evidences a marked resemblance in general to the plain adopted by the Republican national conventions.

Procedure in the Convention. The first national Republican convention held in Philadelphia, June 17th, 1856, was opened by the Hon. Edwin D. Morgan of New York, with the following words: "Delegates of the National Convention, representatives of the heart and hope of the Nation, the day and hour appointed for

[1] *Journal of the National Republican Convention which assembled at the City of Baltimore December 12th, 1831, for the nomination of candidates to fill the offices of President and Vice-President.* Three of the four great committees of the present day conventions were appointed, also temporary and permanent officers similar to the more modern practice.

this gathering have arrived and in behalf of my associates of the National Committee, I now call this assemblage to order." "Thus the body to which pertains
the supreme authority in a great political organization
was formally called into being by the action" of the
national committee, appointed by the antecedent Pittsburg gathering. "It at once entered upon its duties
and assumed all the powers and privileges belonging
to such a body. A resolution was adopted providing
for the appointment of a national committee, consisting of one member from each State and Territory to
serve during the ensuing four years. "All our information goes to show that this was in the minds of the
people the accepted form of organization." [1]

From the beginning, Republican national conventions have been "called to order," usually about noon
of the day appointed in the call, by the chairman of the
national party committee. After the reading of the
official call,—which in the earlier conventions was done
by the chairman, but after the first few conventions became the duty of the secretary of the national committee,[2]—the proceedings of each day's session (usually
a forenoon and an afternoon sitting) are opened with
prayer by some clergyman of local eminence, "the
susceptibility of various denominations being duly respected in the selection." [3] This has been the invariable
rule since the days of the preliminary Pittsburg con-

[1] Professor Macy's statement that this was a "self-constituted" national committee is apparently an error. *Vide, Party Organization
and Machinery,* 68.

[2] Thus in the convention of 1888 the chair announced simply: "The
Secretary will read the call for the Convention."

[3] See the official proceedings of the various Republican national
conventions.

vention of 1856 when the Reverend Owen Lovejoy opened the proceedings with prayer.

Everything in the convention is done according to strict rule, with a scrupulous observance of small formalities. "Points of order,[1] almost too fine for a parliament, are taken, argued and decided on by the chairman to whom everyone bows."

The proceedings of the previous conventions have always served as a model to the succeeding conventions (the minutes of the preceding convention frequently lying open before the chairman during the session). It was of course, however, some years before precedents became definitely established and practice settled according to rule.[2]

The national committee, either before or after the opening prayer and perhaps a short address by its chairman, reports either through him or its secretary a list of the temporary officers of the convention, consisting of a temporary chairman, one or two secretaries and several (six or eight) assistant secretaries and

[1] See *Official Proceedings of the Convention of 1868* relative to Grant's nomination as a typical example.

[2] "The Chairman—What is the further pleasure of the Convention with regard to the earliest possible permanent organization? Divers committees I find were appointed at the last convention, the proceedings of which I have before me. I think the next business which was transacted four years ago, was the calling of the States for the purpose of selecting a committee to report officers for the Convention. Is it the will of the meeting that the States should be now called for that purpose?" (Charles W. Johnson's *Proceedings of the First Three Republican National Conventions* reprinted by order of the Republican National Convention of 1892, of which Mr. Johnson was secretary.)

reading clerks together with a sergeant-at-arms and one or more official stenographers. The earliest illustration of a part of this practice was the appointment of John A. King of New York to act as temporary chairman [1] at the Pittsburg convention, after Lawrence Brainerd of Vermont, one of the signers of the famous Washington call of January 17, 1856, and probably the chairman of the committee composed of the Republican State committee chairmen previously mentioned, had read the call. In 1860, the chairman of the national committee again named Hon. Robert Emmet for temporary president. Mr. Morgan put the question to the convention, which responded *viva voce* by a unanimous aye. This differed from the custom in later conventions, in which the rule seems to be that, unless the chairman of the national committee recognizes objection on the floor of the convention, the temporary organization announced by the national committee has been adopted by the convention. In the absence of objection, the chairman then appoints two delegates as a committee to conduct the president *pro tem* to the chair.

The nomination made by the national committee is usually accepted by the convention without contest or division. If there is opposition, however, any delegate is entitled to place another name before the convention and call for a vote, or some one may do so as the representative of the minority of the national committee.

The list of temporary officers named by the national committee is usually adopted by the convention, as a

---

[1] See *supra,* page 31.

matter of course, for the business of the temporary organization is largely formal, though the nomination of the temporary chairman is often regarded as the "keynote" to the proceedings. But there have been occasions on which the convention has refused to accept the nominees of the national committee. The first of these occurred at the eighth Republican national convention at Chicago in 1884.[1] In concluding the short opening address, the Hon. Dwight M. Sabin, chairman of the national committee, said:

In conclusion, gentlemen, and at the request of the National Republican Committee, I have to propose to you as Temporary Chairman of this Convention, the Hon. Powell Clayton of Arkansas.

Henry Cabot Lodge of Massachusetts then said:

In accordance with the vote of the majority of the committee and in accordance with precedent, you have presented the name of a gentleman as temporary chairman. It is the right of this Convention to adopt that suggestion, or to revise it, if they deem it to be their duty to do so. With no view of introducing any personal contest * * * but simply with a view to making a nomination for temporary chairman which shall have the best possible effect in strengthening the party throughout the country, there are many members of this convention, I believe, who feel that a nomination which would strengthen the party more could be made than

[1] Full details of the convention are set forth in *Official Proceedings of the Republican National Conventions, 1884-1888* as compiled by Charles W. Johnson, secretary of the Republican national convention of 1900, and reprinted by authority of the Republican national convention of the year; *All the Republican National Conventions,* compiled and edited by Henry H. Smith; Stanwood's *History of the Presidency;* A. K. McClure, *Our Presidents and How We Make Them;* Curtis, *The Republican Party,* II, 116, *et seq.*

that which has been presented by the National Committee.
I therefore have the honor to move, as it is certainly most
desirable that we should recognize as you have done, Mr.
Chairman, the Republicans of the South * * * I move
you, Mr. Chairman, to substitute the name of the Hon. John
R. Lynch of Mississippi.[1]

A debate then ensued upon the question as to
whether the national committee or the convention itself should choose its temporary chairman. The former
had done so unchallenged since 1856. George William
Curtis of New York, answering Mr. W. W. Morrow of
California, who had defended the action of the national
committee, said:

This is the supreme council of the Republican party.
Here at this moment, sir, American citizens professing the
Republican faith are met to open the great Republican campaign of 1884 * * *
Unquestionably it has been the usual practice, as the
gentleman from California (Mr. Morrow) has said, that the
nomination of temporary chairman made by the National
Committee should be ratified by the Convention itself * * *
When, sir, this Convention, without in the slightest degree
impugning the purpose or the authority of that committee,
within its bounds, proceeds to exercise its own unquestionable right to be judged in the first act of the campaign by its
own unquestionable and responsible action, then, sir, this
Convention may rightfully, and with perfect respect recon-
sider the nomination which has been submitted.

A short discussion followed, during which Theodore
Roosevelt of New York said:

Mr. Chairman, it has been said by the distinguished
gentleman from Pennsylvania (Mr. Stewart), that it is with-

[1] *Official Proceedings, etc.,* page 6.

out precedent to reverse the action of the National Committee. Who has not known numerous instances where the action of a State committee has been reversed by the State convention? Not one of us but has known such instances. Now there are, as I understand it, but two delegates to this Convention who have seats on the National Committee; and I hold it to be derogatory to our honor, to our capacity for self-government, to say that we must accept the nomination of a presiding officer by another body; and that our hands are tied, and we dare not reverse its action.

Now, one word more. I trust that the vote will be taken by individual members· and not by States. Let each man stand accountable to those whom he represents for his vote. Let no man be able to shelter himself behind the shield of his State.[1]

After a further discussion, the roll of delegates was called and the nominee of the national committee was defeated by a vote of 424 against 384 and the nomination of Mr. Lynch was then, on motion of the defeated candidate, made unanimous.[2]

Throughout the debate not a word was said about the real matters involved. There was a sharp line of division in the party on the question of whether James G. Blaine should be the presidential candidate, Mr. Clayton the nominee of the national committee for temporary chairman was known to be a supporter of Mr. Blaine and "the opposing section of the party made an alternate nomination." Mr. Lynch the choice of the convention was a colored delegate from Mississippi. Both sides were in accord "that the South

[1] Curtis', *The Republican Party*, II, 118-119 and *Official Proceedings etc.*, page 10.

[2] Though the committee's candidate was defeated, yet the convention after all nominated James G. Blaine.

should be honored with the position" and the supporters of Mr. Lynch maintained that their "candidate
was more fairly a representative of the Party in that
section than Mr. Clayton." No direct criticism of the
committee was made.[1]

In 1888, there was slight opposition also to the
nomination for temporary chairmanship made by the
national committee but, as it was only on the part of
the delegation from Kansas, it was of no serious moment.[2]

When the temporary officers have been installed,
the chairman delivers a speech. After the procedure
in the convention had become somewhat settled, it was
customary, next in the order of business to offer a
resolution, which was usually adopted, that the convention be governed by the rules of the preceding national convention or of the House of Representatives,
"until otherwise ordered."

The Four Great Committees of the Convention. After
the adoption of the resolution pertaining to the rules, a
motion is made and carried for the appointment of the
four great committees of the convention, viz: a Committee on Credentials, a Committee on Permanent Organization, a Committee on Rules and a Committee
on Resolutions, each consisting of one member from
each State and Territory represented in the convention.

Remembering, as we must, that the mechanism of
the Republican party was "patterned or fashioned
after that of the Whig party," it is not surprising
to note that the so-called "great committees of the
convention," which from 1860 onward became fixed

[1] See *Official Proceedings, etc.,* page 22.
[2] See *Official Proceedings, etc., 1888,* page 15.

and permanent features of the Republican national conventions are to a degree to be found in the national convention of the Whig party [1] (or National Republicans as they were then called), at Baltimore, December 12th, 1831, to which we have previously referred, as the prototype in procedure and practice of all those great periodical party assizes.

At that time the first problem which came before the national convention was the matter of credentials, rules, platform and permanent organization. Certain of the committees to report on these questions were appointed by the chairman and others were elected by the delegates to the convention. There appears to have been no special committee on rules. The selection of each committee was made separately at that time, all the members of one being chosen or appointed first and then those of the other committees in due turn.

Three stages may be noticed in the election or appointment of the members of these several committees, viz: in the earlier times in Republican national conventions when they were appointed entirely by the chairman; a second stage when they were elected separately by the delegations to the convention, pursuant to separate resolution, each delegation selecting one of its members for the particular committee; and finally in later times, (the existence of the committees having become a firmly established fact and their names and choice definitely decided upon) when a resolution would be offered somewhat as follows:

[1] *Journal of the National Republican Convention which assembled in the City of Baltimore, December 12th, 1831, for the nomination of candidates to fill the offices of President and Vice-President.*

Resolved: That the roll of the States and Territories be now called and the Chairmen of the different delegations respond with the names of the members selected to serve on the committees on credentials, permanent organization, rules and order of business, platform and resolutions.[1]

When the first preliminary Republican convention assembled at Pittsburg, February 22nd, 1856, Hon. Lawrence Brainerd requested John A. King of New York to act as temporary chairman. One of the first things Mr. King did after making a short address and calling on the Reverend Owen Lovejoy for a prayer, was to appoint a committee on permanent organization, by selecting for it one member from each State and Territory represented in the convention. He also in the same manner appointed a committee on address and resolutions.[2] There was no committee on credentials as the delegates were volunteers and though called delegates represented no one but themselves. There was no committee on rules and order of business.

Proceedings were conducted in a very loose manner, and the actions of the convention were more like those of an enthusiastic mass meeting. However, the committee on organization through its chairman reported permanent officers for the convention, for pres-

[1] *Proceedings of the 8th Republican National Convention held at Chicago, Ill., June 3, 4, 5, 6, 1884,* printed by order of the convention.

It is interesting to note that in State conventions these committees are usually appointed by the presiding officer of the convention without consulting the delegates from the various counties or districts.

Resolutions almost identical in form and substance with the above have been presented at every Republican national convention since 1884.

[2] This differed materially from the subsequent practice of having each State delegation name its representative on the committee.

ident, Francis P. Blair of Maryland, and vice-presidents, one from every State and Territory present, and the committee on address and resolutions through its chairman reported a stirring platform or address to the country.

At the first regular national convention of the Republican party at Philadelphia in 1856, as we have seen, three resolutions were adopted covering the appointment of the committees on credentials, rules and order of business, platform and permanent organization. As to the committee on permanent organization, the resolution proposed "a committee of one from each State and Territory selected by the several delegations" represented in the convention "to report officers to this Convention for its permanent organization"; as to the committee on platform and resolutions that a committee chosen in the same manner "prepare a platform of principles to be submitted to the people of the United States and that all resolutions or papers offered in the Convention in relation thereto be referred to this committee without debate"; the questions of credentials and rules and order of business were covered by a resolution referring both duties to one committee [1] chosen in the same manner as the other committees and instructed to "report the number, names and post-office address of each delegate together with rules for the government of the Convention." It was also resolved that no ballot be taken for President or Vice-

---

[1] This practice has never been followed since. The committee on credentials is always separate from the committee on rules and order of business.

President until after the platform had been reported and adopted.[1]

The committee on permanent organization, selected pursuant to the resolution quoted above, reported a list of officers for the convention consisting of a president, Col. Henry S. Lane of Indiana, and a vice-president and a secretary from each State and Territory represented. This was a departure from the practice at the Pittsburg convention, for there only vice-presidents had been reported.

The committee on platform and resolutions reported a preamble and series of resolutions to constitute the platform of the convention.

At the second national Republican convention, held at Chicago in 1860, separate resolutions were moved and carried, first that a committee consisting of one delegate from each State and Territory represented at the convention be elected by the delegates thereof, who should report officers to the convention for a permanent organization; second, that a committee, similarly elected, be formed for the purpose of reporting to the convention the number, names and post-office addresses of the delegates and acting as a committee on credentials; and third that a committee chosen in like manner should report rules for the government of this convention; and fourth that a committee similarly chosen be formed to constitute a committee on resolutions.

The appointment of these committees according to

---

[1] This has become a permanent practice in all Republican conventions and is re-enacted at each convention not as a resolution but as one of the rules reported at each convention by the committee on rules and order of business.

the resolutions finished the first day's work of the convention.

In the convention of 1864, the chairman kept before him a copy of the proceedings of the preceding national convention and, at his suggestion, the appointment of a committee was moved as follows:

Resolved: That a Committee composed of one delegate from each State be appointed for the purpose of receiving a list of the delegates and deciding who are entitled to be present.

This was merely a repetition of the motion made in 1860, but an important amendment was suggested by and carried on the motion of Mr. J. H. Lane of Kansas, to the effect that the delegates from States in which there were contests should not be permitted to participate in the appointment of a committee on credentials.[1] This principle was embodied either in the resolutions or practices merely of several later conventions [2] until 1888. At the convention of that year the chairman stated that the national committee had placed certain delegations upon the roll as *prima fiacie* entitled to seats and that unless the convention should otherwise determine the chair would hold that for the purposes of participation in the temporary organization these delegations alone had the "right to name the committees and to vote." A motion to adopt a resolution similar to that of 1864 above mentioned

[1] At this time Missouri was specially mentioned.

[2] For 1868 see *Official Proceedings, etc., 1868*, pp. 10, 17; for 1872 see *ibid.*, 1872, p. 125; for 1876, see *ibid.*, 1876, p. 238; for 1880, see *ibid.*, 1880, pp. 385, 386; for 1884, see *ibid.*, 1884, p. 27.

was voted down but the convention carried the following:[1]

Resolved: That the roll of States and Territories be called for the presentation of credentials and for notice of contests, and that all such papers be referred without statement or debate to the Committee on Credentials.

This resolution was never again adopted by any convention but the principle has been acquiesced in and the list of delegates as prepared by the national committee has without question always been accepted for the purposes of temporary organization. [2]

The convention of 1864 also carried the resolution of Mr. Creswell of Maryland that the States which had reported the name of a delegate selected for the committee on credentials should be called again in order that one member might be designated from each State to constitute a committee for the permanent organization of this convention.

A similar resolution was carried in order to constitute a committee on platform and resolutions.

At this convention also Mr. A. K. McClure of Pennsylvania, chairman of the committee or permanent organization, reported a list of officers, which report was adopted. It named William Dennison of Ohio for president, and one vice-president from each of the 23 States represented and one secretary also from each of these States, following precisely the practice of the preceding convention and establishing the precedent which has been followed without change ever since.

[1] See *Official Proceedings, etc.,* 1888, p. 33:

[2] See *infra,* Chapter IV.

No committee on rules and order of business had been appointed so far at the convention of 1864. This had escaped the attention of the delegates, as the following extract from the official proceedings will show:

The President * * * "I observe to-day that no Committee was appointed on the order of business. Such a Committee is indispensable to the end that a rule may be established as to the manner of voting and various other questions that will have to be considered. If some gentleman of the Convention will be so kind as to submit a motion for the appointment of such a Committee, the Chair will take great pleasure in submitting that motion to the Convention.

The motion was made and carried and a committee for that purpose, chosen in a manner similar to the others, was appointed.

At the convention of 1868, four separate resolutions were made and carried for the appointment, by the delegates of each State and Territory present, of one of their members to each of the four great committees. The same rule without exception was followed at the conventions of 1872, 1876 and 1880.

Although not officially recognized until 1884, it had become the custom for the chairmen of the different State delegations to give to the secretary of the convention the names of the four representatives from each State, at the same time. In 1884, the resolution was carried that "the roll of the States be called and the chairmen of the different delegations respond with the members of the Committees on Credentials, Permanent Organization, Rules and Order of Business and Platform and Resolutions." From that time the chairmen of the different delegates have presented all the names at one time.

Generally speaking, the committee on rules has little more to do than to adopt the rules and orders of the last preceding convention and submit them to the convention where they may be amended if it is found desirable,[1] but the work of the committee on credentials is, as we shall see, much more complicated and elaborate.

The appointment of the committees and the reference of the various resolutions presented to the appropriate committees end the regular work of the first day's session; the remainder of the time being taken up in deciding with regard to the admission of spectators, in passing resolutions of sympathy for distinguished men as the occasion requires, in listening to addresses by prominent visitors[2] and in dealing with other comparatively unimportant matters.

The Work of the Committee on Credentials. During the recess of the convention, the committees continue at their work. The committee on credentials is hearing the evidence and listening to arguments in the cases of contested seats, for this committee must report at the next session if possible, the names of the delegates who are entitled to sit and vote in the convention.

After the second session of the convention has been called to order by the temporary chairman, the reports

[1] *Official Proceedings of the Republican National Convention, held at Chicago, June 3d, 4th, 5th and 6th, 1884,* page 30.

[2] Thus in 1876, Mrs. Sarah Jane Spencer delivered a short address on "Woman Suffrage," the first introduction of that weighty problem in a Republican national convention.

of the various committees are heard. In the convention of 1856, no definite rule regarding the order in which the reports should be heard was adopted, but, at the convention of 1860, the rule was passed that "the report of the Committee on Platform and Resolutions shall be acted upon before the convention proceeds to ballot for President and Vice-President." In 1864, a rule was passed as follows: "The report of the Committee on Credentials shall be disposed of before the report of the Committee on Platform and Resolutions is acted upon, and the report of the Committee on Platform and Resolutions shall be disposed of before the convention proceeds to ballot for candidates for President and Vice-President," and this has been incorporated in the rules adopted at each succeeding Republican national convention.

At the second session of the convention, the first business in regular order is the report of the committee on credentials. Inasmuch as, properly speaking, no business can be transacted until the committee on credentials has made its report, if that committee is not ready when the convention assembles on the morning of the second day, the convention either adjourns until the following day or, if the report is likely to come in at any moment, the time of waiting is occupied with the offering of various resolutions by different delegates. These resolutions are generally referred without debate to the committee on resolutions. Occasionally [1] the time is devoted to listening to the report of the committee on rules if it happens to be

---

[1] *Proceedings of the Republican National Convention Held at Chicago, etc., 1880,* pp. 419, 420.

ready first, discussion thereof and action thereon being
deferred until after the adoption of the report of the
committee on credentials.

The delay of the committee on credentials in reporting does not postpone the permanent organization
of the convention. This may be effected with the un-
derstanding that those may vote on questions relating
to permanent organization who hold the certificates of
membership in the convention issued by the secretary
of the national committee. Whether some of these
are subsequently displaced by the report of the credentials committee may be determined later, but it
must however be decided before the more important
business of the convention is transacted.[1]

The usual delay in the report of the committee on
credentials is due to the large number of contested
seats. For instance at the Republican convention of
1892, there were twenty-four separate cases and, with
the exception of the convention of 1856, there have
never been less than a dozen contests. "When we consider that several months are often spent by congressional committees in the consideration of contested
election cases it is not to be wondered at that the
committee of a national convention, intrusted with a
similar duty, is sometimes two or three days in ar-

---

[1] In 1872, the rules were on motion suspended and the candidate
for President nominated and ballotted for before the committee on
platform reported. This was an exceptional case. It was Grant's second nomination. There was apparently no other aspirant in the
field and Grant was unanimously elected on the first ballot, receiving
the vote of every delegate from every State and Territory represented, a total of 752 votes.

riving at a conclusion in regard to all the cases before it."[1]

In the matter of the admission of delegates, the proceedings of the earlier conventions were most irregular, but in 1868, several notices of contested delegations were filed in advance with the national committee and in time this practice became universal and established.[2] At length in 1884, it was formally sanctioned by a rule to that effect which was embodied in the call[3] and has been repeated in all the following ones.

All notices of contests between delegations are now filed in advance with the national committee, (pursuant to the provisions of the call) which makes up the temporary roll and these documents relative to the several disputes are then passed on to the committee on credentials which holds meetings, hears the contesting delegations and prepares its report. After both sides have had an opportunity to present their claims, the committee decides between them. The "regular" delegate or delegates, that is, those endorsed by the State or district committee usually receive the seats, especially if there is but one or two contested cases from a State. "Where, however, there are two full delegations from the same State and the contestants on each side appear to have a strong case, it is usual for the sake of harmony and to avoid open rupture to give seats to both delegations, each member being entitled to half a vote. Such contests are often exceedingly bitter because the two delegations

[1] Dallinger, *Nominations to Elective Office,* 81.

[2] See as an illustration *Official Proceedings, etc.,* 1880, page 385.

[3] See *supra,* page 102.

support rival candidates for the presidency and consequently the report of the committee on credentials frequently has an important bearing" on subsequent nominations. The report, which consists of decisions in regard to all contested seats together with an official list of all the delegates entitled to seats in the convention arranged by States, is usually accepted by the convention without much debate.

"Occasionally, however, especially in the later Republican conventions, the committee's report has given rise to a heated discussion" and not infrequently on division of the committee the recommendation of the majority has been rejected. Sometimes these contests are very exciting, for the policy of the party on national issues and the fate of candidates may be decided by the admission or rejection of certain delegations. Perhaps the most exciting contest of this kind occurred at the Republican convention which nominated Garfield in 1880.[1] This discussion of contested seats takes up over one hundred pages of the published proceedings, and led to the ultimate adoption, as we have seen,[2] of uniform rules for the election of delegates.

The following extracts from the report, presented by the committee on credentials to the Republican national convention of 1884, may be taken as typical of the general form of report, usually offered by the committee:

[1] *Proceedings of the Republican National Convention held at Chicago, Illinois, June 2d, 3d, 4th, 5th, 7th and 8th, 1880*, pp. 420-523.

[2] *Supra*, pages 99 and 100.

To the President and Members of the National Republican
    Convention—*Gentlemen:*

Your Committee on Credentials respectfully report that
they met for organization on the evening of June 3d instant,
and selected Hon. Henry Ballard, of Vermont, as their
Chairman and Edwin C. Nichols, Esq., of the State of Michigan, as Secretary, and proceeded to the consideration of the
contests in this body.

Your committee report that they annex hereto the printed
roll of membership prepared by the National Committee
with the changes therein made by your committee. As to
the several contested cases, your committee report upon each
as they have considered them, as follows:

First: In the case of the First District of Alabama, the
Committee find the sitting members, James E. Slaughter and
Frank H. Threet and their alternates as on the roll of the
National Committee entitled to their seats.

Ninth: In the case of the Nineteenth District of New
York, the committee recommend that the sitting delegates,
George Campbell and Hiram Griggs with their alternates,
Andrew S. Draper and Madison Covert, and the contestants,
James Lamb and James A. Houck, with their alternates,
William H. Haskell and Nathan D. Wendell, be each ad-
mitted to seats in the Convention with one-half a vote to
each delegate.

Tenth: In the case of the Twenty-first District of Pennsylvania, the committee find the sitting member [there was
a contest only as to one member] James E. Sayers with his
alternate entitled to his seat.

Eleventh: In the case of the contest of the State of Virginia, the committee by a unanimous vote find that the delegation from said State, headed by Senator William Mahone,
are each [*sic*] and all entitled to their seats in this Conven-

tion in accordance with the roll of delegates and alternates as made up by the National Republican Committee.

Twelfth: In the case of the Fifth District of Kentucky, the committee recommend that the sitting members Silas F. Miller and John Mason Brown with their alternates, John Barrett and August Kahlert, and the contestants, Augustus E. Wilson and Michael Minton and their alternates, Hugh Mulholland and George W. Brown, be each admitted as delegates and alternates to this Convention with the right to cast one-half a vote each. This recommendation is consented to by the sitting members and contestants.

All of which is respectfully submitted.

HENRY BALLARD, *Chairman.*

EDWIN C. NICHOLS, *Secretary.*

To this report is attached a list of the delegates and alternates with the post-office addresses of each, the States being named in alphabetical order and the district delegates and delegates at large being separately enumerated.

The Work of the Committee on Permanent Organization. After the report of the committee on credentials has been finally disposed of, or if it be found necessary to grant the committee on credentials more time, the temporary chairman calls for the report of the committee on permanent organization. This committee reports the long list of permanent officers of the convention previously arranged to a greater or less extent by the national committee, consisting of a permanent chairman or president, a list of vice-presidents and a corps of secretaries, one from each State and Territory represented. If these nominations are accepted, and the report is usually adopted as a matter of course, the temporary chairman appoints a committee of two to escort the permanent chairman [1] to the platform.

The permanent chairman or president [2] as he is usually called, on taking the chair, proceeds to deliver a carefully prepared speech congratulating the party, urging harmony and wisdom in the party councils, and reviewing and defining the issues,—in brief sounding a keynote for the approaching campaign. After the delivery of this address he is then sometimes presented with a gavel. [3]

The Rules and the Work of the Committee on Rules. Next, in the order of business, comes the report of the committee on rules, which consists of an order of business for the convention, together with the rules of the preceding convention amended in such ways as the

[1] While the nomination of the temporary chairman may be regarded as the "keynote" to the proceedings, "he is not called upon to make any important decision from the chair which may affect the platform of the party or its nominations. The duties of the permanent chairman, on the other hand, are most important. He is constantly called upon to decide points of a highly technical nature. He must hold the convention well in hand to prevent it from degenerating into an uncontrolled mob. He is often compelled to choose from among five or ten speakers trying to get the floor at the same time and it is therefore important that he should be master of the rules of procedure and capable of prompt and firm decision."

[2] Sometimes chairman, sometimes permanent chairman, president or permanent president. It varies in the different conventions.

[3] Usually by some State delegation or business concern. See *Official Proceedings, etc.,* 1884, p. 44.

At the national convention of 1888, the delegation from Michigan presented to the temporary chairman of the convention a gavel made from the wood of the oak under which the Republican party is said to have been organized on July 6th, 1854, at Jackson, Michigan. See page 16, *supra,* and note 4.

committee may choose to suggest. The rules in principle are those of the House of Representative with some modifications.

It is customary to adopt a set of rules and order of business at each convention and, until they have been adopted, the convention is governed by the rules of the preceding national convention and the rules of the House of Representatives.

In the case of Republican conventions, very important changes have frequently been made in the rules from convention to convention. "On the other hand, Democratic conventions are traditionally conservative, and the same rules are usually adopted with practically no change." [1]

Conventions have from earliest days been governed by rules of procedure of their own making. At the first regularly constituted Republican national convention at Philadelphia in June 1856, the joint committee on credentials and rules for the government of the convention reported the following "Resolutions for the government of the proceedings of the Convention":

Resolved: That, in voting for a candidate for President, the States be called in their order and that the chairman of each delegation present the number of votes given to each candidate for President by the delegates from his State, each State being limited in its votes to three times the number of electors to which such State is entitled; *Provided* that no State shall give a larger vote than the number of delegates

---

[1] It has always been the practice of Democratic conventions to adopt the rules of the preceding convention without stating specifically what those rules are. This practice has led to much confusion (*Official Proceedings of the Democratic National Convention of 1884*, p. 9, note.)

actually present in the convention; and *Provided* that Kansas shall be considered for this purpose as a State with the same electoral votes as any other State entitled to only one representative in Congress.

Resolved: That the same rule shall apply to the nomination of Vice-President.

Resolved: That the rules of the House of Representatives be adopted so far as they are applicable to this convention.

The rules adopted by the convention of 1860 have been previously detailed.[1] They covered under five heads the following:—(1) the order in which the States and Territories should be called in voting upon subjects before the convention, (2) the basis of voting in the convention and the method of reporting such vote, (3) the adoption of a platform previous to the nomination of a presidential and vice-presidential candidates,[2] (4) a majority of the whole number of votes represented in the convention as necessary to the nomination of candidates and (5) the rules of the House of Representatives as the governing law of the convention.

More numerous and elaborate than the preceding were the rules reported by the committee on the order of business in 1864 as follows:

Rule 1. Upon all subjects before the Convention the States shall be called in the following order: Maine, New Hampshire, Vermont, Massachusetts, Rhode Island, Connecticut, New York, New Jersey, Pennsylvania, Delaware, Maryland, Missouri, Kentucky, Ohio, Indiana, Illinois, Michigan, Wisconsin, Iowa, Minnesota, California, Oregon, West Virginia, Kansas and other States and Territories declared by the Convention entitled to representation in the same shall be

[1] See *supra,* pages 69, 70.

called in the order in which they are added by the Convention.

Rule 2. Four votes shall be cast by the delegates-at-large of each State and each Congressional district shall be entitled to two votes. The votes of each delegation shall be reported by its chairman.

Rule 3. The report of the Committee on Credentials shall be disposed of before the report of the Committee on Platform and Resolutions is acted upon and the report of the Committee on Platform and Resolutions shall be disposed of before the Convention proceeds to ballot for candidates for President and Vice-President.

Rule 4. That when it shall be determined by this Convention what States and Territories are entitled to representation in this Convention together with the number of votes to which they may be entitled, a majority of all the votes so determined shall be requisite to nominate candidates for President and Vice-President.

Rule 5. When a majority of the delegations from any two States shall demand that a vote be recorded, the same shall be taken by States, the secretary, calling the roll of States in the order heretofore stated.

Rule 6. In a recorded vote by States the vote of each State shall be announced by the chairman of the respective delegations and in case the vote of any State shall be divided, the chairman shall announce the number of votes cast for any candidate or for or against any proposition.

Rule 7. That when the previous question shall be demanded by a majority of the delegation from any State, and the demand seconded by two or more States and the call sustained by a majority of the convention, the question shall then be proceeded with and disposed of according to the rules of the House of Representatives in similar cases.

Rule 8.   No member shall speak more than once to the same question, nor longer than five minutes with [out] the unanimous consent of the Convention.

Rule 9.   The rules of the House of Representatives shall continue to be the rules of this Convention so far as they are applicable and not inconsistent with the foregoing rules.

The committee on order of business further recommended and reported the following:

A National Union Committee shall be appointed to consist of one member from each State, Territory and District represented in this Convention.   The roll shall be called and the delegation from each State, Territory and District shall name a person to act as a member of said committee.

The foregoing set of rules have become with slight variations the basis of the rules of all subsequent Republican national conventions.   We trace now the more important variations and changes.

In 1868, in place of rule 1 of 1864, we find the following:

Rule 1.   Upon all subjects before the convention, the States shall be called in alphabetical order.[1]

This has not been departed from.

Another new rule, to check stampeding in the convention,[2] was adopted in that year, which has likewise become a definitely fixed principle, as follows:

Rule 4.   In making the nominations for President and Vice-President, in no case shall the calling of the roll be dispensed with.   When it shall appear that any candidate has received the majority of the votes cast, the President of the

[1] A precedent for this practice existed in the procedure of the National Republican or Whig Convention at Baltimore in 1831.

[2] See *infra,* page 177.

Convention shall announce the question to be, ''Shall the nomination of the candidate be made unanimous''? But if no candidate shall have received a majority of the votes, the Chair shall direct the vote to be again taken, which shall be repeated until some candidate shall have received a majority of the votes cast.

With regard to limiting the time of each speaker in the convention, the following rule was adopted in 1868 which is a slight change from that of the preceding convention.

Rule 8. No member shall speak more than once upon the same question, nor longer than five minutes, without the unanimous consent of the Convention, except that delegates presenting the name of a candidate shall be allowed ten minutes to present the name of such candidate.

The rules adopted in 1872 and 1876 were substantially in accord with and similar to the foregoing. In 1872, the second rule, in addition to defining the representation of the States, expressly allowed each Territory two votes. This rule has been re-adopted in all subsequent conventions, but frequently changed so that certain Territories named therein are granted a larger representation than two, as in 1888, when Dakota Territory was given ten delgates and Washington Territory six. A rule was also adopted that after the States had been called in alphabetical order upon any subject before the convention, the Territories should be called next. In 1876, as a further preventative of stampeding.[1] there was added to the regular provision making the calling of the roll in presidential nominations compulsory, the requirement that "when

[1] See *infra*, page 177.

any State has announced its vote it shall so stand until the ballot is announced, unless in case of numerical error." Rule 1 with regard to calling the roll of States and Territories respectively in alphabetical order was amended by a provision that the District of Columbia be added as the last on the list and an amendment was made to Rule 2 so as to expressly give the District of Columbia two votes.

The rules of the convention of 1880, as reported by the committee of which James A. Garfield was chairman, were practically identical with those of the preceding convention save for mere verbal changes and a re-arrangement into what the committee regarded as a more convenient order.

A change of substance was however made by an amendment to the eighth rule which read:

Rule 8. In a recorded vote by States the vote of each State, Territory, and the District of Columbia shall be announced by the chairman and in announcing the vote of any State, Territory or District of Columbia, the chairman shall announce the number of votes cast for any candidate or for or against any proposition, but if exception is taken by any delegate to the correctness of such announcement by the chairman of a delegation, the President of the Convention shall direct the roll of such delegation to be called and the result shall be recorded in accordance with the votes individually given.

The latter part of this rule which definitely repudiated the so-called "unit-rule [1] in Republican conventions merely embodied "the precedents of rulings in all former Republican National Conventions * * * into a plain unambiguous addition to the rules."[2]

---

[1] See *infra*, pages 152, *et seq.*

[2] Speech of General Garfield, *Official Proceedings*, etc., 1880, p. 419.

A further rule was adopted requiring all resolutions relating to the platform to be referred to the committee on resolutions without debate. This practice likewise had been theretofore embraced in the rules only by implication.

An important amendment was added to the usual rule relative to the appointment of the members of the national committee as follows:

Said committee [the National Republican Committee] shall within the next twelve months prescribe a method or methods for the election of delegates to the next National Convention to be held in 1884; announce the same to the country and issue a call for that Convention in conformity therewith; *Provided*, that such methods or rules shall include and secure to the several Congressional districts in the United States the right to elect their own delegates to the National Convention.

A few changes were made in the rules of the convention of 1884. A rule was adopted making Cushing's *Manual* the guide for general parliamentary law to govern the convention in place of the rules of the House of Representatives.

The ten minute restriction in the case of presentation of names of candidates was removed, but no member was to be permitted to speak more than once upon the same question nor longer than five minutes unless by leave of the convention, but the case of the presentation of names of candidates was excepted.

Several important additions were made to the rule regarding the appointment of a national committee as follows:

Rule 10. A Republican National Committee shall be appointed to consist of one member from each State, Territory and the District of Columbia. The roll shall be called and the delegation from each State, Territory and the District of Columbia shall name through its Chairman a person who shall act as a member of such committee; provided that no person shall be a member of the committee who is not eligible as a member to the Electoral college.[1] Said committee shall issue the call for the meeting of the National Convention, six months at least before the time fixed for said meeting; and each congressional district in the United States shall elect its delegates to the National Convention in the same way as the nomination of a member of Congress is made in said district; and in the Territories, the delegates to the Convention shall be elected in the same way as the nomination of a delegate to Congress is made; and said National Committee shall prescribe the mode for electing the delegate for the District of Columbia. An alternate delegate for each delegate to the National Convention to act in case of the absence of the delegate, shall be elected in the same way and at the same time as the delegate is elected. Delegates-at-large for each State and their alternates shall be elected by State conventions in their respective States.

[1] Under the law passed by Congress in 1883 (Act of Jan. 16, 1883, C. 27, 22 U. S. Stat., 403, §§11, 14) commonly known as the *Civil Service Act,* a provision has been enacted that no person holding a Federal office shall directly or indirectly receive or solicit a contribution, assessment or subscription of money for any political purpose whatever from any other person holding such office.

Under the Constitution of the United States, Article II, Section I, no person holding a Federal office can be a member of the Electoral College.

This addition to the usual rule in 1884 was made through the recommendation of the national committee itself. It has never been adopted at any subsequent convention. *See Official Proceedings of the Republican National Convention held at Chicago June 3d, 4th, 5th and 6th, 1884,* at pages 79 and 80.

An order of business was provided for by Rule 12 which read:

Rule 12. The Convention shall proceed in the following order of business: Commencing after the reports of the Committees on Credentials and Rules:

First: Report of the Committee on Platform and Resolutions.

Second: Presentation of Candidates for President.

Third: Balloting.

Fourth: Presentation of Candidates for Vice-President.

Fifth: Balloting.

This likewise had not heretofore been embraced in the rules of the convention except by implication.

The only significant change made by the rules of the convention of 1888 was the addition of the following:

Rule 11. The Republican National Committee is authorized and empowered to select an Executive Committee to consist of nine members who may or may not be members of the National Committee.

Instead of Cushing's *Manual* as the guide of parliamentary procedure, the rules of the House of Representatives as far as applicable were adopted, returning to the custom of all previous Republican national conventions excepting that of 1884.

Another change, though not a material one, was in a rule excluding from the section of the hall, set apart for delegates to the convention, everybody excepting the delegates themselves and officers of the convention.

It is evident from this review that there has been remarkably little change in the procedure of Republican national conventions during the last fifty years.

There are, however, one or two rules, the history of which is worthy of special notice.

The Democratic Convention at Baltimore, in 1832 adopted certain rules which had a most important bearing upon the procedure in future national party gatherings. The first of these was the following resolution:

Resolved: That each State be entitled in the nomination to be made of a candidate for the Vice-Presidency,[1] to a number of votes equal to the number to which it will be entitled in the electoral college under the new apportionment, in voting for President and Vice-President; and that two-thirds of the whole number of the votes in the convention shall be necessary to constitute a choice.

This was the origin of the famous "two-thirds" rule which has been adopted by each subsequent convention of the Democratic party.[2] Moreover its operation has been confined to that party, a simple majority being sufficient to nominate in both Whig and Republican conventions.

In the Republican national convention of 1860, an interesting debate arose on a proposition to require a vote, equal to a majority of full delegations from all the States, to nominate candidates for President and Vice-President, which, in view of the number of delegates actually in attendance (four hundred sixty-six), would have been about equivalent to a two-thirds rule.

---

[1] There was no opposition in the Democratic party to the nomination of General Jackson for a second term but the party were not so well satisfied with Mr. Calhoun, the Vice-President, so a convention was called to nominate a candidate for the second office.

[2] The two-thirds rule seems to be obsolete in Democratic State conventions except those of Tennessee and Texas and to be confined solely to national conventions.

As originally reported to the convention, by the committee, Rule 4 read as follows:

Rule 4. Three hundred and four votes, being a majority of the whole number of votes when all the States of the Union are represented in this convention, according to the rates of representation presented in Rule 2, shall be required to nominate the candidates of this convention for the offices of President and Vice-President.

A minority report was presented with the following substitute:

Rule 4. That a majority of the whole number of votes represented in this convention according to the votes prescribed by the second rule shall be required to nominate a candidate for President and Vice-President.

It was urged in favor of the majority report that in view of the language of the call of the convention, all the States of the Union were represented "in spirit," and as the chairman of the majority of the committee stated it:

If any State is not represented, whether it be by accident or design, we count her as present. She is here in spirit, she is here in contemplation of the Call of the convention; and we can say she had her rights here, if we can say that our candidates were nominated by a vote they would have had had she and her sisters been here looking to their duties. This was the first view that controlled a majority of the committee,—that a precedent might be set here and now that to nominate a Republican candidate should require a delegate for each elector that it would take to give him a bare majority in the electoral college.

Mr. James of New York, as chairman of the minority committee urged in part the following:

When this question arose in the committee the report of which is now presented, there were but seventeen members of that committee present, ten being absent and upon the sense of that body being called they stood nine to eight,— nine for the majority and eight against it. You will thus see the difference between the two reports. One is substantially the "two-thirds rule." If there are 466 votes, 311, I believe is two-thirds of that vote, and this rule requires 304. Therefore it is only seven short of the two-thirds rule which has been adopted by the Democratic party in the management of their conventions. I am not aware that any such rule was ever adopted by any party in opposition to that party and I was not aware that that party ever adopted that rule until * * * it became necessary for the interests and purposes of slavery that the minority should rule the majority. For that reason I am opposed to that rule. I have sufficient confidence in the integrity and judgment of this convention to trust the nomination of its candidate to the majority of the delegates here.

And Mr. Mann of Pennsylvania further added:

I come here from a land where we acquiesce in the will of the majority on all questions when men are invited together to deliberate. I know nowhere in a Republican convention where men are entitled to vote by proxy.

The proposition presented by a majority of the committee was voted down and the convention decided by a vote of 358½ to 94½ that only a majority of those present should be required to nominate candidates. In 1864 again a majority of those present was required but in 1868 the convention enacted a rule making a "majority of the votes cast" the required number to nominate for President and Vice-President and this has been the rule [1] without exception of all subsequent Republican national conventions.

Another resolution [2] adopted by the Baltimore convention of 1832, which was of great future significance, was as follows: "That in taking the vote the majority of the delegates from each State designate the person by whom the votes of that State shall be given." This was the origin of the famous "unit rule." Although several of the State delegations were divided in this convention, nevertheless the rule tended (as the result of the balloting showed) to bring it about that the majority of each delegation decided for whom the entire vote of the State should be cast.

In 1839, the unit rule was adopted by the Whig party. At the national convention of that year, a resolution was carried that each State delegation should vote by itself for the candidates for Presidency and Vice-Presidency, and that "the vote of the ma-

[1] Carl Becker, *"The Unit Rule in National Nominating Conventions."* *American Historical Review*, Oct., 1899, V, 64. See also Stanwood, "Election of 1844," and Niles, vol. lxvi., p. 211 ff., cited in Mr. Becker's article. See also Dallinger, *"Nominations for Elective Office in the United States,"* Harvard Historical Studies, 1897.

[2] The two-thirds rule, though in its origin no part of the unit rule is really very closely connected with it. "The first Democratic convention adopted this rule because it was believed that nominations thus made would have greater authority with the people." ("The Unit Rule in National Nominating Conventions." C. Becker, *American Historical Review*, V, 64.) As the prestige of the National Convention increased and the two-thirds rule was no longer required for this purpose it was retained, as the debates show especially in 1844 (Niles LXVI, 211, *et seq*), to supplement the unit-rule which many States were employing, as it lessened the probability that a few very large States which were nearly evenly divided on candidates and yet enforced the unit rule "might secure a majority for a can-

jority of each delegation should be reported as the vote of that State," in a sort of committee of the whole. The decision of the committee of the whole was then to be reported to the convention.[1]

Either in the form of a rule adopted by the convention or in the form of instructions by the State convention, this practice of having a majority of each State delegation control the entire vote of the State soon became more or less fixed in the procedure of both of the leading political parties of that time.

The unit rule "is one which allows (but does not compel) the majority of a State delegation to cast the entire vote of the State." It restricts the right of the individual delegates to vote according to their preferences; the State convention, whether it elects only the four delegates-at-large or all the delegates, can order them to vote in a body at the national convention in accordance with the decision of the majority.[2] For instance, if in the State delegation of seventy-two members, instructed to vote as a "unit," thirty-seven delegates are in favor of a certain candidate, the votes of the other thirty-five delegates are placed to his credit although they are hostile to him.

didate whose actual strength would measure only a small minority." (Becker, *American Historical Review, supra.*)

[1] For the rule see Niles, LVII, 249, *et seq.,* cited by Becker, *supra.*

The rule is said to have been the culmination of a shrewd scheme to defeat Henry Clay. (Von Holst, *Constitutional History of the United States,* II, 361-369; Benton, *Thirty Years' View,* II, 204.)

[2] It is really not a rule of the national convention but of the individual delegations;—being their manner of voting, their way of casting the ballots of the State which they represent; it concerns the national convention only so far as that body sanctions or does not sanction the practice on the part of the State delegations.

In Democratic conventions, where the convention of a State has instructed the delegation to vote as a "unit" or where the chairman of the delegation so announces it and it is not challenged by a delegate, the entire number of votes to which the State is entitled in the convention is cast by the chairman for one candidate.[1] Otherwise the chairman announces the number of votes cast for each candidate in the poll of the delegation. It is left to the States concerned to adopt or reject the principle as they see fit; but if the State does not act in the matter, the delegates may vote as individuals.[2]

Like the two-thirds rule, the unit rule applies only in the Democratic conventions. The Republicans have never used it;[3] that is, it was never knowingly tolerated, in the Republican national conventions. No minority, as we shall see, ever made a protest against the

---

[1] This is in line with the general Democratic conception of the representation of the State as being of a highly centralized character. For a discussion of the advantages of the Republican and Democratic practice in this regard, see C. A. Beard's *American Government and Politics,* 171, 172. The reasons for the difference between the Democratic and Republican practice are also ably treated in C. Becker, "The Unit Rule in National Nominating Conventions," *American Historical Review V,* 80 et seq.

[2] *Official Proceedings of the Democratic National Convention of 1904.*

[3] Mr. Dallinger is apparently in error (*Nominations for Elective Office in the United States,* pp. 41 and 134) when he says that it became fixed in the Republican party, and the first "successful revolt against this disregard of the right of the minority occurred in the National Convention of the Republican party in 1876" and "was abandoned by the Republicans in 1880." This inaccuracy is also noted by Mr. Becker in *American Historical Review,* V, 65, 80.

use of the unit rule in the Republican convention which was not sustained. Republican state conventions have repeatedly tried to introduce the rule, but the national conventions, beginning with that of 1856, on each occasion admitted the right of each individual delegate to cast his vote as he chose, under all circumstances.

In the first Republican national convention in 1856, the committee on credentials, which also reported rules, recommended that in voting for candidates "the chairman of each delegation present the number of votes given to each candidate for president by the delegates from his state * * *." No question could well arise as to the proper interpretation of a rule so clearly set forth as this, and as far as the official proceedings show none did arise.

In 1860 different rules were reported and the manner prescribed for the casting of votes was less definite. "Four votes," so runs the rule, "shall be cast by the delegates at large of each state and each congressional district shall be entitled to two votes. The votes of each delegation shall be reported by its chairman." On the first ballot for President under this rule Maryland voted eleven for Bates. A delegate objected on the ground that the Maryland delegation had not been instructed to vote for Bates. The chairman of the delegation, explained that the State convention had at first instructed the delegation, but later had changed the instruction to a mere recommendation. It was on the force of this recommendation that he had announced the vote as eleven for Bates. The chair then ruled that the announcement of the chairman of the delegation must be accepted unless the convention decided otherwise. He therefore put the question to the convention:[1] "Shall the vote announced by the chairman be received by the convention as the vote of the State of Maryland?" The question was decided in the negative; it is not stated by how large a majority.

In the national convention of 1864 the rule on the casting of votes was substantially re-enacted as follows:

Rule 6. In a recorded vote by States, the vote of each State shall be announced by the chairman of the respective delegations and in case the vote of any State shall be divided, the chairman shall announce the number of votes cast for any candidate or for or against any proposition.

The two subsequent conventions made no change in the rule for the casting of votes save that in 1872 a slight change in phraseology was introduced.[2]

"The year 1876 marks the appearance of a desire among certain Republicans to introduce the Democratic custom of disregarding the rights of the minority into their party." The Louisiana delegation at its meeting just previous to the convention resolved according to State instructions to force a unit vote on the delegation.[3] In the New York meeting we are told

[1] *Official Proceedings*, 1860, pp. 150-151.

[2] The rule is as follows: Rule 2, Each State shall be entitled to double the number of its Senators and Representatives * * * according to the recent apportionment. * * * The votes of each delegation shall be reported by its chairman. (*Official Proceedings*, 1872, p. 144. For 1864 see *Official Proceedings*, pp. 201-2. For 1868 see *ibid.*, 1868, p. 43.

[3] New York *Tribune*, June 14, 1876.

that the "attempt of some of the Conkling men to enforce a unit vote failed." [1]   And the Pennsylvania State
convention gave the following instructions to its delegates:[2] "upon all questions to be brought before or
arising in the convention to cast the vote as a unit as
a majority of the delegation may dictate." In the
national convention itself, however, the rule which the
committee reported was apparently clear in its opposition to any unit voting, reading as follows:

> In the record of the votes by States the vote of each State
> *   *   *   shall be announced by the Chairman and in case
> the votes   *   *   *   shall be divided, the Chairman shall
> announce the number of votes cast for any candidate or for
> or against any proposition.

Despite this fact, Pennsylvania seemed determined
to stand by her instructions and her action raised objections which lead to a somewhat extended discussion.
During the progress of the balloting for President, the
fifty-eight votes of the delegation were cast by that
State for Hartranft of Pennsylvania for President; but
two delegates desired to vote for Blaine and rose to a
question of privilege and demanded that their votes
be thus separately recorded.[3]   The chairman of the
convention, Mr. McPherson, sustained the demand of
the two Pennsylvania delegates under the sixth rule of
the convention and decided "that it is the right of

[1] New York *Tribune*, June 13, 1876.

[2] *Ibid.*, June 14, 1876.

[4] *Political Manual of 1880; Proceedings of the Republican National
Convention held at Cincinnati, Ohio, 1876.* (Officially reported by
W. A. Clancey of Washington, D. C., 1876, Concord, N. H., printed
by the Republican Press Association.)

any and every member equally to vote his sentiments in the convention." An appeal was taken from this ruling but his decision was sustained by the convention by a vote of 395 to 354.[1]

"The Louisiana delegation evidently receded from the position taken in its preliminary meeting, for the vote of that State was divided throughout."

The only serious attempt to introduce unit voting into the Republican conventions was made in 1880. This was not done because the rule was desirable, but because its use would serve the special ends of certain political leaders. A desperate effort was made to nominate General Grant for a third term. Senator Conkling of New York, Senator Cameron of Pennsylvania and Senator Logan of Illinois were leading the wing of the Republican party, the "Old Guard," that proposed the nomination of General Grant and "set themselves to work to give their candidate the prestige of an undivided vote from those States." [2] As the third term doctrine was very unpopular this could only be done by shrewd management. In Pennsylvania and New York, conventions were held early and unit instructions were passed with no great difficulty, but in Illinois it was not so easy. The Grant men secured control of the State convention and the chairman appointed a committee to report a list of delegates to the national convention. The practice

---

[1] Curtis, *The Republican Party*, II, 58.

[2] Becker, *American Historical Review*, Oct., 1899, V, pp. 78-80.
See also the very interesting account in A. R. Conkling, *Life and Letters of Roscoe Conkling*, 588-609; also New York *Tribune*, May 14, 1880.

had been for the delegation from each district in the
State to appoint its own national delegate; but the
new plan of a committee left them no choice and resulted in a solid Grant delegation from Illinois.
Similar tactics apparently had been used in many of
the county conventions previously. Besides these States,
several others also instructed their respective delegations to vote as a unit for General Grant.

This started a revolt in many States. Indignation
meetings were held in Illinois and an anti-Grant delegation was also sent to the convention.[1] Many of the
delegates from New York and Pennsylvania, as the
time drew near declared their intention not to abide
by the instructions which they had received,[2] but the
"leaders continued in their determination to nominate
General Grant by forcing the unit rule upon the convention. Their plan was somewhat as follows": the
chairman of the national committee, Senator Cameron, was to call the convention to order and present
the temporary chairman, whom that committee had
selected, to the convention. If a Grant man was chosen,
he was to rule that all the delegations which were
under State instructions to vote as a unit, must abide
by those instructions. If an anti-Grant man was
named (which might be the case since the national
committee was thought to have a majority opposed to
Grant), someone was to move to substitute the name of
a Grant man in his stead and in the ballot Senator
Cameron would enforce the unit rule on all instructed
States. In this way the supporters of General Grant

[1] New York *Tribune*, May 27 and June 5, 1880.
[2] *Ibid.*, May 5 and 6, 1880.

hoped to organize the convention, but they never got that far. The question was fought out before ever reaching the convention, in the preliminary meeting of the national committee. It turned out that about twenty-nine of the committee were anti-Grant men; and fully aware of the scheme to force the unit rule on the convention, they presented the following resolution to the committee when they met:[1]

Resolved, That the Committee recognize the right of each delegate in a Republican National Convention freely to cast and to have counted his individual vote therein according to his own sentiments, and, if he so decide against any unit rule or other instructions passed by a State convention; which right was conceded without dissent and was exercised in the conventions of 1860 and 1868, and was after full debate confirmed by the convention of 1876; and has thus become a part of the law of Republican Conventions and until reversed by a convention itself must remain a governing principle.

"The adoption of such a resolution would be fatal to Senator Cameron's plans and he knew that a majority of the committee were in favor of it, because the twenty-nine anti-Grant members had held a caucus the evening before in which they had denounced the practice of unit voting and had agreed to present such a resolution to the committee when it came together. He therefore resolved upon the bold step of refusing to put the question when the resolution was offered and declared everyone out of order who tried to appeal from his decision. His action led to a storm of denunciation and the anti-Grant men of the com-

[1] Becker, *American Historical Review*, V, 78, and New York *World*, June 1, 1880, cited by Becker, *ibid.*

mittee prepared to remove the Senator from the chairmanship; but rather than submit to this he yielded
and a compromise was effected. The unit rule was not
enforced in the temporary organization and the Senator
was permitted to retain his position as chairman. This
ended the matter. The convention organized quietly,
with the anti-Grant men in control." [1] Garfield was made
chairman of the committee on rules and the rule which
he drew up then with reference to balloting by States,
and which he claimed but embodied "the precedents
of rulings in all former Republican conventions," [2] has
been retained by Republican conventions ever since.
"It is a model of precision and makes unit voting impossible except in cases where the minority neglects or
refuses to make any objection." It is as follows: [3]

Rule 8. In the record of the vote by States, the vote of
each State   *   *   *   shall be announced by the chairman,
and in case the vote of any State   *   *   *   shall be divided,
the chairman shall announce the number of votes cast for
any candidate or for or against any proposition; but if
exception is taken by any delegate to the correctness of
such announcement by the chairman of his delegation, the
president of the convention shall direct the roll of members
of such delegation to be called, and the result shall be
recorded in accordance with the votes individually given.

No attempt was made by either Cameron, Conkling
or Logan [4] to cast the votes of their respective States

[1] Becker, *American Historical Review*, V, 78; New York *Tribune*,
June 1, 1880.

[2] *Official Proceedings of the Republican National Convention, etc.,
1880*, p. 419.

[3] *Ibid.*

[4] The Grant delegation from Illinois was unseated by the committee
on credentials. (*Official Proceedings, etc., 1880*, p. 428.)

as a unit, and the votes of those States were divided from the first ballot. In fact at Mr. Conkling's own suggestion the roll of individual delegates of the States of New York was called after the first ballot and the divided vote of that State then announced. Of the Southern States which had been instructed, Alabama, Kentucky and Texas cast divided votes on the first ballot.[1] Arkansas voted solidly for Grant throughout.

During the convention apparently the only question having any relation to unit voting was raised by the State of Michigan. The vote was on directing the committee on rules to report. Mr. Joy stated that one of the delegates from Michigan was on the committee of credentials, and wished to know if the delegation had the right to cast his vote in his absence knowing how he would vote. But the chair decided against even this.[2]

Thus in 1880 the consistent practice of the Republican party "was crystallized in a rule which secured future conventions from all attempts of a similar nature" to that made in the convention of 1876. And it has been the constant policy of the Republican party ever since (as was again illustrated in 1888) to allow each delegate to cast his vote as he pleased, not only as

[1] Mr. Becker is apparently in error when he states (*American Historical Review*, V, 79) "Of the Southern States which were uninstructed, Alabama, Kentucky and Texas cast undivided votes on the first ballot." The error is two-fold. The delegations of Alabama and Texas were instructed. (*Vide*, Mr. Becker's own article at page 77 and New York *Tribune*, May 28, 1880) and their votes were divided from the start. (*Vide, Official Proceedings of the Republican Nation Convention*, etc., 1880, pages 567, 568.)

[2] *Official Proceedings*, etc., 1880, p. 408.

against unit voting, but even as against the instructions of his district or State convention.

The "unit-rule," the "two-thirds rule" and the
method of apportionment of delegates without regard to
relative party strength have been called the three evils
of the national convention because generally not found
in State conventions. The reason lies probably in the
fact that the latter are nearer to the people and "less
influenced by tradition and precedent than are the national party councils."

*The Platform and the Work of the Committee on
Resolutions.* Having been permanently organized and
the membership having been fixed, the convention then
proceeds to consider the platform reported by the committee on resolutions.

Declarations of party principles naturally accompanied the nomination of party candidates and so the
party platform had its origin. As in the case of the
convention system, the germ of the platform may be
traced a long way back. In 1800, the congressional
caucus of the then Republican party adopted resolutions setting forth the principles represented by Jefferson's candidacy; and later congressional caucuses followed this practice. In 1812, the New York legislative
caucus which nominated Clinton for the Presidency
set forth the grounds of opposition to Madison in a
series of resolutions. During the Jackson movement,
the adoption of resolutions at meetings and conventions
became a regular practice. When national party conventions regularly assumed the function of selecting
candidates, they could not well avoid making state-

ments of party principles. Public opinion demanded such explanations and the politicians were forced to yield.

The National Republican or Whig party which met at Baltimore in 1831 and nominated Clay, issued an appeal[1] to the voters referred to as "The first platform ever adopted by a National Convention." Most of the succeeding conventions followed this example; and never, since the first national convention of the Republican party in 1856, has any party failed to submit to the people some declaration of its purpose.

The Democratic declarations of 1840 may be said to be the first that involved the three essential factors of a modern platform,—a statement of fundamental party principles, policies to be pursued under the pending circumstances, and pledges that these principles and policies would be carried out. Before this there were addresses adopted at public meetings and conventions, resolutions approved by ratification meetings, criticisms or defences of the administration published by party leaders, which were generally accepted as the basis of party action; but these were not platforms in the prevailing modern sense.

The first so-called platform of the Republican party, adopted in the Pittsburg convention of 1856, to which we have previously referred,[2] differed from all subsequent ones in that it concluded with a sort of "call" for the Philadelphia convention of the same year, in addition to the "Declaration of principles"

[1] "Address of the National Republican Convention to the People of the United States," see *Journal of the National Republican Convention, etc., 1831,* p. 113.

[2] See *supra,* page 36 and footnote to that page.

for which unity in political action was sought by the new party.

It differed also in that it bore a long title, viz: "Address of the First Republican National Convention, held at Pittsburg, Pa., February 22nd, 1856; Declarations of Principles and Purposes which we seek to promote," and because of its extreme length, for it consisted of eleven very closely printed pages.

The platform, adopted by the convention held at Philadelphia in 1856, consisted of a preamble and series of resolutions, nine in number, each resolution beginning with the word "Resolved."

At this early stage the Republican party, owing to the Whig element whose influence was felt, inserted a plank in its platform favoring internal improvements, but nothing was said about the tariff.

The history of the Republican party is a singular commentary upon its first declaration of principles at Philadelphia in 1856. There is in that declaration no direct reference to slavery in the States, nor to slavery in the District of Columbia nor to the rendition of fugitives from service.

The platform of 1860 was most carefully and accurately drawn. While clearly asserting the fundamental Republican propaganda it at the same time aimed to conciliate as wide and varied elements as possible. [1] It is worthy of note that (with the exception of the platform of 1876,—the centennial year) this is the

---

[1] It said nothing directly of the Fugitive Slave Law, or the abolition of slavery in the District of Columbia.

only platform which re-affirmed the principles of the Declaration of Independence, which the reader will doubtless recall were inserted at the suggestion of Joshua Giddings, aided by the eloquent efforts of George William Curtis. The platform began with the words "Resolved" and then followed a series of seventeen declarations in which it was stated the delegates united.

In 1864, Henry J. Raymond of New York presented on behalf of the committee on resolutions a platform [1] consisting of eleven resolutions most of which referred to the issues growing out of the war. Some reference was made, however, to a Pacific railroad, the currency and the Monroe Doctrine. This platform had no preamble and each of its eleven resolutions began with a number and with the word "Resolved."

A short heading prefaced the platform of 1868 [2] as follows:

The National Union Republican Party of the United States assembled in National Convention in the City of Chicago, on the 21st day of May, 1868, make the following declaration of principles.

The platform itself consisted of fourteen declarations of principles, each beginning with a number, the salient feature being perhaps embodied in number two as follows:

[1] The full text of the platform may be found in Curtis, I, *The Republican party*, 436, and in Charles W. Johnson's *Proceedings of the First Three Republican National Conventions*.

[2] The full text of the platform may be found in Curtis, *The Republican party*, I, 502-504, and in *Proceedings of the National Union Republican Convention held at Chicago, May 20th and 21st, 1868*, reported by Ely, Burnham and Bartlett, Official reporters of the convention (Chicago, 1868).

The guarantee by Congress of equal suffrage to all loyal men at the South, was demanded by every consideration of public safety, of gratitude and of justice, and must be maintained; while the question of suffrage in all the loyal States properly belongs to the people in those States.

The platform of 1872,[1] unlike the preceding platforms, for the first time in the history of the Republican party, was not an aggressive battle-cry. As the party of achievement, its duty was to preserve what had been gained. This was declared in a long and elaborate platform of nineteen paragraphs each beginning with a number. After a short preamble in which the party appealed to its history, it "announced its position upon the questions before the country." It was pledged to promote complete liberty and exact equality in the enjoyment of all civil, political and public rights by appropriate federal and State legislation; it claimed for the recent constitutional amendments that they should be supported because they were right; it took strong ground in favor of a reform of the Civil Service; it favored protection for American industries; it opposed further land grants to corporations, approved additional pensions, and justified Congress and the President in their measures for the suppression of violent and treasonable organizations in the South.

[1] The full text of the platform may be found in Curtis, *The Republican Party*, II, 24, and in *Proceedings of the National Union Republican convention held at Philadelphia, June 5th and 6th, 1872, which nominated for President and Vice-President, Grant and Wilson*, reported by Fancis H. Smith, Official Reporter, and printed by Gibson Bros., Printers (Washington, 1872).

The declaration of principles, eighteen in number (each beginning with a number), which formed the platform of 1876, [1] started with a lengthy preamble reaffirming the cardinal truths contained in the Declaration of Independence, suggested by the centennial year.[2] It recognized the pacification of the South and the protection of all their citizens as a sacred duty; the enforcement of the Constitutional amendments was enjoined and the obligation of removing any just cause of discontent was coupled with that of securing to every American citizen complete liberty and exact equality in the exercise of all civil, political and public rights. The platform also favored a more radical reform of the Civil Service; the extirpation of polygamy was demanded and an investigation into the Chinese question then beginning to distract California, was recommended.

The platform of 1880[3] differed in form from all

---

[1] For the full text of the platform, see Curtis, *The Republican party,* II, 53, and *Proceedings of the Republican Convention,* held at *Cincinnati, Ohio, June 14, 15, 16, 1876, resulting in the nomination for President and Vice-President of Rutherford B. Hayes and William A. Wheeler.* (Officially reported by W. A. Clancey, Washington, D. C., 1876, Concord, N. H., printed by the Republican Press Association.)

[2] This patriotic appeal in the Republican platform of 1876 may also be due to the fact that "the Republican party emerged from the period of Reconstruction during which the Southern States were restored to their former position in the Union as a reorganized party fortified by the devotion of an intense patriotism." (Beard, *American Government and Politics,* 117.)

[3] For the full text of the platform see *Political Manual of 1880,* edited and compiled by Stiles & Hutchins, 74 *et seq.;* Curtis, *The Republican Party,* II, 78, and *Proceedings of the Republican National*

preceding ones.   The party was no longer an infant but
was fully grown and proud of its career, and its
platform which the committee on resolutions through
its chairman, Mr. Edwards Pierrepont of New York,
submitted to the convention, began as follows: "The
Republican party in National Convention assembled,
at the end of twenty years since the Federal Government was first committed to its charge, submits
to the people of the United States this brief report of its administration."   Then follows a list of
"past performances," among others the suppression
of the rebellion, the reconstruction of the Union, the
liberation of four million human beings, the abolition
of slavery, restoration of the currency to a solid
basis, improvement of the credit of the nation, the
vast increase in the railway system, foreign trade and
exports of this country, the reduction of the public
debt, etc., and, "upon the record, the Republican party
asks for the continued confidence and support of the
people and this Convention submits for their approval
the following statements of the principles and purposes
which will continue to guide and inspire its efforts."
Then follow seven such statements of principles closing
with a scathing denunciation of the Democratic party.

The platform of 1884,[1] as reported by the chairman

*Convention held at Chicago, Ill., June 2, 3, 4, 5, 7 and 8, 1880, result-
ing in the nominations of James A. Garfield and Chester A. Arthur.*
(Officially reported by Eugene Davis and printed at Chicago, Ill., 1881.)

[1] For the full text of the platform, see Curtis, *The Republican
Party*, II, 127, and *Official Proceedings of the Republican National
convention held at Chicago, June 3, 4, 5 and 6, 1884*, reprinted by authority of a resolution of the Republican National Convention of 1900
at Philadelphia, by Charles W. Johnson, Secretary of that convention
(Minneapolis, Minn, 1903.)

of the committee on resolutions, William McKinley of Ohio, was the longest and most elaborate as well as the most complete of any we have hitherto discussed. It began proudly

1. The Republicans of the United States, in National Convention assembled renew their allegiance to the principles upon which they have triumphed in six successive Presidential elections, and congratulate the American people on the attainment of so many results in legislation and administration by which the Republican party has, after saving the Union, done so much to render its institutions just, equal and beneficent.

It contained twenty-two paragraphs each one numbered consecutively and concluded as follows:

22. We extend to the Republicans of the South, regardless of their former party affiliations, our cordial sympathy, and pledge to them our most earnest efforts to promote the passage of such legislation as will secure to every citizen, of whatever race or color, the full and complete recognition, possession and exercise of all civil and political rights.

This marked the beginning of the long, detailed and elaborate platforms which have followed in the Republican party and was the last year in which each paragraph was numbered or, as we have seen in many instances, began with the word "Resolved." After 1884, the arrangement of the platform bore either no marking of paragraphs at all by way of consecutive numbering or resolution, or else was topical as *e. g.,* in the platform of 1900, "Currency,—We renew," etc.; "Trusts,—We recognize," etc.; "The war in South America—we commend," etc.

The platform,[1] then, as we have seen, is an address to the people consisting some times of various "planks," or a series of resolutions, sometimes of an address without division into numbered sections but always containing the principles and programme of the party. Generally speaking, "it usually contains among other things references to the great history of the party interspersed with the names of party leaders and denunciations of the policies and tactics of the opposite party." It arraigns the opposing party for its errors, criticises it for its course of action, joins issue with it on prominent policies before the public and gives promise as to what the party will do if elected or retained in power. In the platforms, the managers usually try to conciliate every section of conflicting party opinion and frequently produce a document which treats with "prudent ambiguity," the questions upon which there may be division in the party. The part which this conjuring away of the problems of the day has played in political contests is significant. Only on exceptional occasions, at times of grave crises which distracted the party, when there was no opportunity for evasion, has the platform met the question of the day with a straight-forward answer; but apart from cases of this kind, the principal object of the platform is, in the present day as formerly, to catch votes by trading on the credulity of the electors.[2]

In the Democratic convention at Charleston, in

[1] All the national platforms of the Republican party from 1856-1908 are printed in Tweedy's *History of Republican National Conventions.*

[2] As was aptly said "And thus each mighty party engaging in the bout, for fear of being beaten will leave the platform out." (New York *Times,* Oct. 3, 1907.)

1860, a debate on resolutions led to a secession and to the break-up of the Democratic party, but of late years the adoption of platforms has been almost a matter of form, the report of the committee being usually a unanimous one.

The reading of the platform is one of the most interesting features of a national convention. The resolutions are read by the chairman of the committee, who is generally one of the leading men of the party and the reading is frequently interrupted by applause. Any delegate who objects to a resolution can move to strike it out or amend it, but it is generally sustained in the shape it has received from the practiced hands of the committee.

The Nomination of Candidates. After the adoption of the platform comes the call of the roll of States, arranged in alphabetical order from Alabama to Wisconsin and then of the Territories in like alphabetical arrangement and lastly the District of Columbia, for the presentation of candidates for the presidential nomination.

This was not the case as we have seen in the earlier conventions, in which the roll of States was called (not merely for the presentation of presidential nominees but for all purposes) according to geographical location.[1] In 1864, there was added to the rule specifying this geographical arrangement of roll call, the provision that after naming all the States and Territories represented in that convention, other States and Territories declared by the convention entitled

[1] Thus in 1856 the roll began with Maine, New Hampshire, Vermont and concluded with Minnesota and the District of Columbia.

to representation in the same "shall be called in the order in which they are added by the convention." In 1868, the rule was adopted that the States should be called in alphabetical order[1] and this has been followed without change.

A representative of a State, which is thus named, thereupon places a candidate in nomination in a speech of high flown eloquence. Reference has already been made[2] to the fact that in the conventions of 1856 and 1860 no nominating speeches were made and the audiences were not thrilled with the brilliant rhetoric and long-winded orations of later years. In 1864, there was a bare resolution that Abraham Lincoln be declared the choice of the party. In 1868, Mr. Logan's speech nominating Ulysses S. Grant occupied but five lines in print, but in 1872, the nominators began to depart from the laconic practice of earlier times. Mr. Shelby M. Cullom in re-nominating General Grant addressed the convention as follows:

Gentlemen of the Convention: On behalf of the great Republican party of Illinois and that of the Union,—in the name of liberty, of loyalty· of justice and of law; in the interest of economy, of good government, of peace and of equal rights for all,—remembering with profound gratitude his glorious achievements in the field and his noble statesmanship as chief magistrate of this Nation, I nominate as President of the United States for a second term Ulysses S. Grant.

And when the tumult of applause which greeted this had ceased, Governor Stewart L. Woodford of New York ascended the platform to second the nomination

---

[1] See *supra,* page 142.

[2] See *supra,* pages 49 and 73.

NOMINATING MACHINERY, 1864-1884

and made a stirring address, concluding with the
words:

In the name of millions of our loyal people, in the name
of an enfranchised race, in the name of his old comrades,
the living and the dead, in the name of the dead Secretary
of War, New York endorses the nomination and asks God's
blessings on the cause.

In the convention of 1876, came the famous nominating address of Robert Ingersoll in naming James
G. Blaine, the "plumed knight" and in 1880, Roscoe
Conkling's equally famous address, nominating General Grant, and Garfield's address, nominating General Sherman. From that time on, the custom was
fixed and, to-day, the nominating speeches are perhaps
the most stirring (and sometimes the most tedious)
feature of the convention.

If a State has no candidate of its own to nominate,
it may yield its position to another further down the
line.[1] If a State has a "favorite son," however slight
his chance of securing the nomination, his name is
likely to be put before the convention; "this custom
makes it possible for a State delegation to pay a compli-
ment to some prominent party leader." After the names
of the candidates have been presented by delegates usually from the State of their birth or residence. "State
delegations, which have no additional candidates of
their own to present, sometimes authorize one of their
number to second in a short speech one of the nominations already made." Frequently nominations are

[1] In the Republican convention of 1904, when Alabama was called
upon the chairman of the delegation said: "The State of Alabama re-
quests the privilege and distinguished honor of yielding its place upon
the roll to the State of New York."

seconded with a view to showing the extent of the candidate's appeal.   Thus, in 1872 when Mr. Cullom of Illinois, the President's own State, nominated Mr. Grant;
and as Horace Greeley of New York was going to oppose
him, it was arranged that Stewart L. Woodford, who
was also from New York, should second Grant's nomination.

The procedure in the convention permits the closing of the nominations without calling the full roll of
States, but if desired the calling of the roll may be
completed.

When the presentation of names of candidates is
concluded, the convention proceeds to the first ballot.
A peculiar procedure was adopted by the convention of
1856 in this respect. A resolution was passed as follows:

Resolved: That this convention proceed immediately
to take an informal vote for a candidate for President of
the United States to be supported by the Republican party of
the United States.

This, as we have indicated in a preceding chapter,
was a substitute for nominations from the floor for
the names of no candidates had been presented as
nominees by the delegates.

The voting then proceeded, and Fremont, receiving
359 votes as against 190 for Judge McLean, was by
resolution "unanimously nominated by this convention
by acclamation as the Republican candidate for President of the United States."

It was then

Resolved: That this convention do immediately proceed to take a formal vote for a Republican candidate for
President of the United States.

On this ballot Fremont received 580 votes as against 37 for his nearest competitor and it was then resolved "that this convention do unanimously nominate John C. Fremont of California to be the Republican candidate."

A similar procedure of informal and formal ballots was adopted for the nomination of Vice-President, but, since that earliest convention of the Republican party, this practice has not been followed and one formal ballot after the other is taken until the requisite majority is obtained.

The vote is taken by calling the roll of States and Territories. As the name of each State is called by the secretary of the convention, the chairman of the State delegation rises in his own place and announces the vote of his own State [1] for each of the candidates named, in case the vote of the delegation is divided. If any member of the delegation challenges the vote as returned by the chairman, the roll of the delegation is called by the secretary of the convention and the delegates vote individually.

---

[1] It proceeds thus, taking the convention of 1868 as an example:

"The Secretary,—the State of Alabama.

The Chairman of the Alabama delegation,—Mr. President, Alabama, through the Chairman of her delegation, casts eighteen votes for U. S. Grant.

The President,—Alabama casts eighteen votes for Ulysses S. Grant." And so on until finally:

"The Secretary,—The State of Wisconsin.

The Chairman of the Wisconsin delegation,—Mr. President, Wisconsin, the last on the roll of states, adds her voice to that of her sister States and gives her sixteen votes for Ulysses S. Grant.

The President,—Wisconsin gives sixteen votes for Ulysses S. Grant and the roll is completed. Gentlemen of the convention, you have 650 votes. You have given 650 votes for Ulysses S. Grant."

If no candidate obtains the requisite majority, which in Republican conventions has always been a majority of the delegates present and voting, the roll is called again, in order that individual delegates may have the opportunity of changing their votes and the process is repeated until some one of the aspirants put forward has received the required number of votes. Sometimes a considerable number of ballots must be taken before the requisite majority is obtained. Thus in 1880, thirty-six ballots were taken before James A. Garfield was declared duly nominated, the proceedings occupying two whole days. When no aspirant is able to command at the start, a majority of the whole convention, each endeavors to arrange a combination, whereby he may gather votes from the supporters of other nominees. "The breathing space between each ballot and that which follows is used by the managers for hurried consultations. * * * One balloting follows another until what is called the 'break' comes. It comes when the weaker factions perceiving that the men of their first preference cannot succeed, transfer their votes to that one among the aspirants whom they like best or whose strength they see growing. When the faction of one aspirant has set the example, others are quick to follow and thus it may happen that, after thirty or forty ballots [1] have been taken with few changes of strength as between the two leading competitors, a single ballot, once the 'break' has begun and a column of one or both of these com-

---

[1] There have been few cases in which the candidate obtained a majority at the first ballot, as Cleveland and Harrison in 1892. On the other hand in several cases, the number of ballots has been very large; Garfield was nominated in 1880 on the 36th ballot; Pierce in 1852 on the 49th and Scott in 1852 on the 53rd ballot.

petitors has been 'staggered,' decides the battle. But if two well matched rivals have maintained the struggle through twenty or thirty ballots, so that the long strain has wrought up all minds to unwonted excitement, the 'break' when it comes, comes with fierce intensity. The defeat becomes a rout, and battalion after battalion goes over to the victors while the vanquished ashamed of their candidate, try to conceal themselves by throwing away their colors and joining in the cheers that acclaim the conqueror. In the picturesquely technical language of politicians it is a stampede."[1]

In 1864, before the final vote was announced, Missouri which had cast its 22 votes for Ulysses S. Grant, changed them to Lincoln, and at the same convention, in the balloting for the Vice-Presidential candidate, there was a change of many States even on the first ballot before it was announced, so that Andrew Johnson received 494 votes, as against 26 for all other nominees.

To prevent a recurrence of this practice, the Republican convention of 1868, as we have seen, adopted a rule providing that the roll of States should in no case be dispensed with. This makes surprise and tumult less dangerous..[2] With the same object in view, the Republican convention of 1876 ruled that no vote given on any balloting should be changed before the end of that balloting.

Each ballot is followed with the utmost anxiety by

[1] Bryce, *American Commonwealth* (abridged edition, 1900), pp. 475, 476.
[2] Stanwood's *History of Presidential Elections*, 174, 369, 468.

the whole assembly and invariably gives rise to noisy demonstrations. In accordance with the custom of other parties, the practice in the Republican conventions from the earliest day, when the result of the final ballot has been announced has been to make the nomination of the candidate unanimous. At the convention of 1868 this was for the first time made a part of the rules themselves, as follows:

Nominations for President and Vice-President shall be made by calling the roll and this shall be repeated until a candidate have a majority of the votes cast, when the President of the Convention shall announce the question to be "shall the nomination of the candidate be made unanimous?"

Whether embodied in the rules of the convention or not, this has been followed in all subsequent conventions, though frequently in the enthusiasm of the moment, the motion is put before the chairman's question is asked. The chairman need not wait for any motion but may put the question immediately upon the announcement by the secretary.[1]

The practice and procedure for the selection of the

[1] Thus at the convention of 1884 at the conclusion of the fourth ballot:

The President: James G. Blaine, of Maine, having received the votes of a majority of all the delegates elected to this convention, the question now before the convention is, "Shall the nomination of Mr. Blaine be made unanimous. On that motion the Chair recognizes Mr. Burleigh, of New York.

Mr. Burleigh, of New York: Mr. President, In behalf of the President of the United States, and at his request, I move to make the nomination of James G. Blaine unanimous.

The following extract from the proceedings of the convention of 1880 is significant:

The President: James A. Garfield of Ohio is nominated for Pres-

candidate for Vice-President, which follows immediately after the nomination of the candidate for President has been made, is exactly the same as that followed in nominating a candidate for the presidency.

After the nominations have been made, usually on the third or fourth day of the session, motions are generally carried empowering the national committee to fix the time and place of the next national convention and to perform other services, in case provision for such matters has not already been made in the rules. Then, after adopting resolutions, providing for the printing of the proceedings of the convention,[1] thanking the citizens of the place where the convention has been held for their hospitality and expressing appreciation to the different officers of the convention for their services, the national convention adjourns *sine die;* the grand council of the party is over. The convention

---

ident of the United States. Shall the nomination be made unanimous?

Mr. Conkling of New York. *Mr. President:* James A. Garfield of Ohio having received a majority of all the votes cast I rose to move that he be unanimously presented as the nominee of the Convention. The chair under the rule anticipates my motion.

[1] This is usually in pamphlet form and a copy is sent to each member of the convention. In addition to the proceedings of the convention, the pamphlet officially edited and printed by each national convention, contains :

    (A) A list of the officers of the convention,—chairman of the national committee, temporary chairman of the convention, permanent chairman, general secretary, sergeant-at-arms, etc.

    (B) List of the Republican national committee members. (One for each State and Territory in the Union and also from the District of Columbia.)

    (C) List of the executive committee of the Republican national campaign committee of the particular year.

    (D) List of Republican congressional committee members.

having made its nominations and put forth its platform, vanishes like "swans which sing their one song
and die." [1]

The delegates, however, go forth throughout the
length and breadth of the land to labor for the success
of the party at the coming election. Even those who
are disgruntled with the results of the convention are
supposed to "wheel into line" and enthusiastically support the candidates whom they have hitherto bitterly
opposed. This does not always happen however; indeed, in 1880, a very pretty question arose in the convention as to whether the delegates were really bound
to support the nominees of the convention.

Roscoe Conkling offered the following resolution: [2]

Resolved: As the sense of this convention that every
member of it is bound in honor to support its nominee whoever that nominee may be; and that no man should hold a
seat here who is not ready to agree.

This was the first time such a resolution was offered in a Republican national convention. Under the
designation of the "Ironclad Pledge" similar resolutions had been offered in other party conventions at
various times in the past. The roll of States being
called on Mr. Conkling's resolution, resulted in 716

(One from every State and Territory in the Union, either a
Senator or Representative.)

(E) List of the chairmen and secretaries of the Republican
State committee. (A committee from each State and Territory in
the Union.)

The proceedings of the earlier conventions contain no reference
to the national, executive, congressional or State committees.

[1] Bryce, *American Commonwealth,* II, 54.

[2] *Proceedings of the Republican National Convention of 1880, etc.,*
p. 410.

yeas and 13 nays, the latter being cast by West Virginia delegates.[1]

Mr. Conkling then moved that the delegates who had voted "that they will not abide the action of the Convention do not deserve and have forfeited their votes in the Convention." This resolution was strongly opposed and the position[2] taken by the West Virginia delegates sustained by numerous speakers among them James A. Garfield.[3] Mr. Conkling then withdrew the resolution before a vote had been taken thereon.[4]

The motive underlying the presentation of these resolutions by Senator Conkling was his ardent desire to have General Grant receive the presidential nomination. It was part of the "third term fight" and was (together with the attempt previously described to introduce the unit rule into this convention) one of the

[1] One of the delegates stated the grounds for his opposition thus: "Mr. President, I feel as a Republican that there is a principle in this question and I will never come into any convention and agree beforehand that whatever may be done by that convention it shall have my endorsement. * * * I always intend to, carry my sovereignty under my hat" (*Official Proceedings, etc., 1880*, p. 413).

[2] General Garfield said that while he regretted the action of those delegates, yet, "when they tell the Convention that by their dissent they did not mean that they would not vote for the nominee of the Convention but only that they did not think the resolution at this time wise, I say they acted right" (*Official Proceedings, etc., 1880*, p. 416).

[3] When Mr. Garfield resumed his seat Mr. Conkling wrote on a newspaper, "I congratulate you as being the dark horse" and passed it to Mr. Garfield (Conkling, *Life & Letters of Roscoe Conkling*, 592).

[4] Mr. Garfield's remarks affected many delegates and, had a vote been taken, Mr. Conkling's resolution would probably have been tabled by a large majority (Tweedy, *History of Republican National Conventions*, 179).

moves of the New York Senator, as leader of the "Old Guard"[1] to secure the presidential nomination for his candidate and insure the convention's support for him thereafter.

While General Grant, who was a popular idol at the time and had just completed his memorable tour around the world had warm and active supporters in nearly every State in the Union, who favored his nomination for the presidency yet this met with serious opposition at the hands of some who were opposed to the idea of a third term [2] and others who favored the candidacy of James G. Blaine. It was to pledge all members of the convention to the support of Grant, should he succeed in being nominated, that Senator Conkling introduced the resolution which at that time was so favored that it was referred to in the convention as "a resolution which needed no advocacy in a Republican convention and ought to pass without opposition."

But, alas, for the fickleness of man,—the same resolution met a totally different fate when offered by Mr. S. W. Hawkins of Tennessee four years later at the national convention of 1884.[3] At this time it was described by Mr. George William Curtis[4] of New York as a "resolution which should never have appeared in

[1] A Grant medal was subsequently struck off for the three hundred and six members of the "Old Guard" who voted for Grant on the 36th ballot.

[2] It was said in his behalf that the argument should have no force for one term (that of President Hayes) would have intervened.

[3] *Official Proceedings of the Republican National Convention held at Chicago, June 3d, 4th, 5th and 6th, 1884,* page 37, et seq.

[4] See *infra,* page 183.

a Republican convention, as unworthy to be ratified by this convention of free men."

There was a sharp line of separation in the Republican party on the question of James G. Blaine's nomination for the presidency and as the followers of Grant had succeeded four years previously in pledging the convention to support the candidate it might nominate "whoever that nominee" might be, the supporters of Blaine attempted the same tactics, but failed. Lacking the eloquent support of Mr. Conkling and meeting with severe criticism and condemnation at the hands of numerous delegates, the resolution was finally withdrawn by its proposer after lengthy and spirited discussion.

Despite the double victory of the anti-Blaine forces in selecting a temporary chairman in place of the nominee of the national committee (to which we have previously alluded[1]) and in defeating the resolution of Mr. Hawkins, the convention nominated Mr. Blaine which resulted in a "bolting" of the ticket by the Mugwumps [2] or Independent Republicans under the leadership of George William Curtis [3] and Carl Schurz, and the election of Grover Cleveland.

At no succeeding Republican convention has an attempt been made to pledge the convention by a resolution of this kind, but the spirit of the resolution may be said substantially to pervade every national convention.

The Notification of Candidates. Either before or

[1] See *supra,* page 122.

[2] *The Nation,* July 24, 1884.

[3] Curtis and his followers had favored George F. Edmunds.

after the making of the nominations, the national convention appoints a committee or committees to notify the candidates of the action of the convention and reques their acceptance of the nomination and their approval of the resolutions adopted.[1] Such committee or committees usually consist of one delegate from each State and Territory, but the method of choosing them has been most irregular. While, as we have seen, the manner of selecting the various other committees of the convention became at an early date definitely established, the practice of selecting the so-called "Notification Committee" did not become fixed until 1892.

In 1856, as we have previously noted, the chairman appointed a committee of nine delegates with himself as the tenth to notify the nominees. In 1860, the committee was formed by the president of the convention and the chairmen of the respective State and Territorial delegations. In 1864, on motion of George William Curtis of New York, the committee was selected by the respective State and territorial delegations, each naming a representative to act thereon. In 1868,[2] the officers of the convention were, on motion of General Daniel E. Sickels of New York, declared to constitute a committee to communicate to the candidates their nomination. A similar practice was followed in 1872. At the three ensuing conventions, the president of the convention appointed one delegate from each State and

---

[1] A practice established as early as 1831 see *Journal of the National Republican Convention, etc.,* p. 11, and the committee there appointed to notify Henry Clay.

[2] For 1868 see *Official Proceedings, etc.,* 1868, p. 109; for 1872, see *ibid.,* 1872, p. 207; for 1876, see *ibid.,* 1876, p. 332; for 1888 see *ibid.,* 1888, p. 234.

Territory together with himself to constitute this committee. In 1888, the convention reverted to the practice of 1864 and the roll was called and each State and Territory named a member for the committee.

It was not until 1892,[1] that the practice became definitely established as follows: two committees on notification of candidates were appointed, one to notify the presidential candidate and the other to notify the vice-presidential candidate, the delegates from the respective States and Territories each naming one representative for each committee.

The so-called notification committee, through its chairman, in an address, notifies the candidate of his selection and submits to him also the declaration of principles of which it is expected he will approve.[2] The candidate replies informally, accepting the honor conferred upon him, with thanks to the committee and to the convention and to the great constituency they represent. Usually he writes a special formal and

---

[1] *Official Proceedings of the Republican National Convention, etc., 1892*, pp. 122, *et seq.*

[2] Thus Senator Lodge as chairman of the notification committee, notified President McKinley at Canton, Ohio, of his re-nomination for the Presidency by the Republican national convention at Philadelphia, June 19th, 1900, as follows:

"Mr. President, this committee representing every State in the Union and the organized Territories of the United States was duly appointed to announce to you formally your nomination by the Republican National Convention which met at Philadelphia, June 19th last, as the candidate of the Republican party for President of the United States for the term beginning March 4th, 1901." Then follows a lengthy address closing "Thus announcing to you, Sir, your re-nomination as the Republican candidate for the Presidency, we have the honor also to submit to you the Declaration of principles made by the National Convention, which we trust will receive your approval."

rather lengthy letter of acceptance as well. These letters of acceptance together with the notification address and the platform are generally printed in the
political hand-book published during each campaign by
the national committee.[1]

In course of time, the notification of candidates and
their reply became an important ceremony and feature
of the campaign. It has always been the custom for
the committee in a body to visit the candidate at his
home and for the chairman, after delivering an address, to present him with a formal letter notifying him
of his selection. In the earlier times, the address of
notification was very simple and brief and was followed
by the presentation of a written communication, advis-
ing the candidate of the action of the convention and
the resolutions adopted, and in response the candidate
would send a short letter of acceptance, thanking the
convention for the honor conferred. In subsequent
years the letter of notification became a mere form and
the chairman, or some particularly representative man
on the committee, would deliver a long address. The
candidate would make a short speech in reply and at
the same time present the chairman with a brief formal
letter of acceptance. This, in recent years, has been
followed by a longer and in many instances very
elaborate document of acceptance forming, in a way, a
second platform enunciated by the party's candidate
as an addition or amendment to the platform adopted
by the convention itself.

Thus in 1860, Mr. Ashmun, president of the convention and chairman of the notification committee, together with the other members of the committee,

[1] See *infra,* Chapter IV.

waited upon Mr. Lincoln at his residence in Springfield, Illinois. The chairman's address was very brief,
and Mr. Lincoln's reply but a few lines in print.[1]   A
written address announcing his nomination was thereafter sent to Lincoln to which he replied as follows:[2]

Springfield, Ill., May 23, 1860.

Hon. George Ashmun,
    President of the Republican National Convention.

Sir:

I accept the nomination tendered me by the Convention
over which you presided and of which I am formally apprised
in the letter of yourself and others acting as a Committee
of the Convention for that purpose.

The declaration of principles and sentiments which ac-
companies your letter meets my approval and it shall be my
care not to violate it, or disregard it in any part.

Imploring the assistance of Divine Providence and with
due regard to the views and feelings of all who were represented in the Convention, to the rights of all the States and
Territories and people of the nation, to the inviolability of
the Constitution and the perpetual union, harmony and pros-
perity of all, I am most happy to co-operate for the practical success of the principles declared by the Convention.

Your obliged friend and fellow citizen,

ABRAHAM LINCOLN.

In 1864 a short address was delivered to which
Lincoln's answer was equally brief, but the letter[3] of
notification (written by George William Curtis) was
long and elaborate, containing a detailed paraphrase

---

[1] Raymond, *Life, Public Services and State Papers of Abraham Lincoln,* 105.

[2] *Ibid;* a facsimile is reprinted in Nicolay and Hay, II, 277.

[3] Raymond, *Life Public Services and State Papers of Abraham Lincoln,* 561.

of the platform. Lincoln's reply, addressed to "Hon. William William Dennison and Others a Committee of the National Union Convention," was but some sixteen or eighteen printed lines in length.[1]

Since 1872, the proceedings of the notification committee have been printed in the official proceedings of the convention as an appendix thereto and also published as a part of the campaign year book. About that time, also, the practice became definitely settled and established of having a short address together with a short formal letter of notification on the part of the committee and on the part of the candidate a short address followed by a short formal letter of acceptance.[2]

In 1876, the letters of acceptance become somewhat more elaborate and Rutherford B. Hayes started the custom of a lengthy letter of acceptance with a discussion of the party platform, stating his views on the currency question and other matters, as did also the vice-presidential nominee, William A. Wheeler.

Already in 1880, we find the letters of acceptance of James A. Garfield and Chester A. Arthur each a little over three closely printed pages in length. Mr. Blaine's letter of acceptance in 1884 covers ten closely printed

---

[1] "In accepting the nomination, the President observed the same wise rule of brevity which he had followed four years before" (Nicolay and Hays, IX, 77); Raymond, *Life, Public Services and State Papers of Abraham Lincoln,* 563.

[2] General Grant in 1872 received the committee at the White House and the various members of it congratulated the President and he said a few words to each instead of making a formal reply. This had never been done before nor has it been followed since.

pages and is a most careful survey and discussion of the political issues of the day coupled with his views upon the principal questions. That of the vice-presidential nominee, General Logan was but a few pages shorter than Mr. Blaine.

In 1892, the practice was inaugurated of having separate committees, one to notify the presidential nominee and the other to notify the vice-presidential nominee. The committee to notify President Harrison of his nomination for a second term, assembled at the Ebbitt House at Washington and then headed by its chairman, Governor William McKinley, Jr., proceeded to the Executive Mansion, where they were met by about 200 invited guests and friends of the President. Lengthy speeches were made on both sides and a luncheon was served at the Executive Mansion to the committee and all the invited guests. President Harrison's formal letter of acceptance covers twelve closely printed pages and is subdivided, the various divisions dealing under different headings with a dozen or more of the political issues of the day such as the currency system, reciprocity, the tariff, etc.

This established the formal precedent and the proceedings and letters of acceptance have become more elaborate with each ensuing year.

Special trains were used to convey the notification committee and invited guests to the proceedings, notifying President McKinley at his home in Canton, Ohio, of his nomination in 1900 and McKinley's letter of acceptance, 24 closely printed pages in length, is second only in length to that of Col. Roosevelt's in 1904, which was about 30 closely printed pages and covered some two dozen political issues and questions of the day to each of which a special subdivision of the letter of acceptance is devoted.

Verily a change from the early simplicity of the days of Lincoln!

CHAPTER IV

THE REPUBLICAN NATIONAL COMMITTEE IN ITS ORIGIN AND DEVELOPMENT

When the curtain falls on the national convention, the first act in the selection of the President and Vice-President is at an end; the nominations made by the rival parties are submitted to the sovereign voters and it is for the latter now to give a decision.

The presidential campaign,—the culminating point, in what an able student of our system describes as our "quadrennial political cycle,"—has arrived.

Hitherto, the contact between party organization and the electorate has been very slight,—merely at the party primaries.[1] Now, "the besieging army supplied by the American party organization prepares for active battle. The national committee of each party, appointed every four years at the national convention, may, to continue our simile, be regarded as the staff of that besieging army, and its chairman, a sort of field-marshal." This committee, unique in its powers

---

[1] "The primary in the various uses of the term serves as an agency for nominating local offices, for selecting delegates to party conventions, for instructing voters, for giving information to party representatives in office as to the views of their supporters and in general for expressing the attitude of the great body of party electors toward the policy of party leaders. The primary is a name given to the original formal act of the voters in setting in motion the machinery of government. In its several uses the word always has reference to the point of immediate contact of the whole body of electors with their government."

and duties, holds a position of the highest importance and responsibility in the party. "It is the one permanent national party institution,[1] which stands for the unity of the entire party, since in its composition every part of the nation is represented."

"The permanent national committee is the one extra-legal institution capable of being called into action for the solution of party questions. The congressional committee,[2] which is also national and of independent origin and development, is yet, from the standpoint of general authority, distinctly subordinate. It is the national committee that embodies the party unity." [3]

One of the earliest national party committees of which we have any record was the committee of correspondence, consisting of one member for each State, appointed by the Republican caucus of 1812 to see that its nominations were duly respected. In 1831, the National Republican or Whig party at its convention in Baltimore formed a campaign committee, composed of one member from each State selected by the delegates to the convention. In fact as early as 1830, it had come to be realized that the existence of national, State, county, district and local committees of the different political parties was conducive to the main-

---

[1] Unlike many countries of the European continent in which the *cadres* of the parties are formed on the eve of the election and break up soon afterwards, their contingents often presenting only floating masses, England and the United States have a form of permanent party organization.

[2] See *infra*.

[3] Jesse Macy, *Party Organization and Machinery*, 40.

tenance of party efficiency.[1]   The building up of this organization was well advanced for the Democratic party about the year 1835, for the Whig party not until some years later.

Although the early national conventions, like the first State conventions, usually elected a committee of correspondence, it was not until the Democratic convention of 1848,[2] that a permanent national committee consisting of one member from each State was choosen, with power to call the next national convention.   The present Republican party, born after the establishment of this precedent and developing on very similar lines the method which experience had approved in other parties, has had a national committee from the beginning of its history.

"The Republican party was locally organized before National agencies were brought into use, [3] and an accredited National Committee appeared before a convention was called to place in nomination a candidate for the presidency.   Among the many local organizations,[4] one under the name of 'The Republican As-

---

[1] Van Buren put the political party on the basis of a conquering army by means of a net work of committees all over the State.

[2] The Democratic convention at Baltimore in 1848 "directed the appointment of a Central Committee of one member from each State to take general charge of the canvass and of the party's interest. This was the first National Committee ever organized." (J. A. Woodburn, *Political Parties and Party Problems in the U. S.,* 199.)

[3] See *supra,* page 22.

[4] One of the most important and significant facts historians tell us connected with the formation of the Republican party is the "spontaneity of the movement and the large number of its independent points of contact with the people." (J. Macy, *Party Organization and Machinery,* 66.)

sociation of Washington, District of Columbia,' was formed, June 19th, 1855. [1] On January 17th, 1856, this body issued a circular, urging Republicans to organize clubs or associations in all cities, towns and villages and giving minute directions as to methods of insuring successful coöperation." [2] In this circular appeared the following significant passage: "We have therefore to request that, should you organize a Republican Association or should there be one already in existence in your place, you will urge upon its members the importance of at once collecting funds for the purpose of procuring and disseminating the proper kind of documents among the masses, either by your association or by our National Committee." "This is probably the earliest reference made to a Republican national committee," but "the title designates here merely a committee of a local association at the capital which assumed the name." [3]

On the same day, January 17th, 1856, there was also issued from Washington, a call signed by the chairmen of the State Republican committees of five States inviting the Republicans of the United States to meet in informal convention at Pittsburg, February 22nd, 1856, "for the purpose of perfecting the National Organization and providing for a National Delegate Convention of the Republican party at some subsequent day to nominate candidates for the Presidency and Vice-Presidency." "The self-appointed body which issued this call did not name itself a National Com-

[1] For details regarding this association see *supra,* pages 23, *et seq.*

[2] Jesse Macy, *Party Organization and Machinery,* 66.

[3] *Ibid,* 67.

mittee, though it might have done so with much more appropriateness than did the local Washington committee," just referred to, "which assumed the name." [1]

At the informal Pittsburg convention which met pursuant to the call above mentioned, the chairman appointed a committee on national organization, by selecting one member from each State and territorial delegation present in the convention and also from the District of Columbia.

This "committee on national organization" was merely a temporary committee of the convention, appointed to devise plans for and make recommendations to the convention in order to help perfect the national party machine.

The committee recommended the holding of a national convention for the nomination of President and Vice-President at Philadelphia on the 17th of June, 1856, and suggested also the representation of the States at that convention together with a plan for the organization of the party throughout the country, including the formation of a "National Executive Committee".

This committee on national organization has never again appeared in any Republican national convention. It was formed to meet the peculiar necessities of the time, namely to get the Republican party under way nationally, and ceased its existence with the special exigencies which required its creation.

The committee on national organization was not the forerunner of the present national committee as it

---

[1] Jesse Macy, *Party Organization and Machinery*, 67.

exists in the Republican party. The origin of this
latter committee is to be found in the "National Executive Committee," which was recommended by the
committee on national organization above mentioned.
Like the others this committee was appointed by the
chairman, who selected one member from each State
and Territory represented in the convention and also
from the District of Columbia. The committee was authorized to add to its number one member from each
State not represented and to fill vacancies. It met at
Willard's Hotel in Washington [1] on March 27th, 1856,
and in issuing the formal call for the first national Republican nominating convention to be held at Philadelphia on June 17th, 1856, it may be regarded as the first
regular Republican national committee.

It entered at once upon its duties and took to itself
large powers and privileges, but these, however, were
a mere shadow compared with the powers its successors
were ultimately to assume, and of which its creators and
members at that time little dreamed. The Hon. Edwin
D. Morgan as chairman called the Philadelphia convention to order as he stated, "in behalf of my associates
of the national committee." After his opening address
he put before the convention the name of a temporary
chairman, and, upon his election appointed a committee of two to conduct that gentleman to the chair.
In the course of the proceedings a resolution was
adopted providing for the appointment of a national
committee, consisting of one member from each State
and Territory represented in the convention to serve

[1] See *supra,* pages 51, 52.

during the ensuing four years. This was apparently the usual form of organization.[1]

At the convention of 1856, also, the problem of where to hold the next national convention came up for discussion and it was finally voted [2] to leave the question to be determined by the national committee. Thus began a precedent significant in its consequences, as we shall see, and followed without exception ever since.

At the convention of 1860 the following resolution was passed, together with an amendment that the delegations should be allowed to select members of the national committee who were not members of the convention:

Resolved: That the delegations from each State and Territory represented in this convention be requested to designate and report the name of one individual to serve as a member of the national Republican committee for the ensuing four years.

This established the method of forming the Republican national committee which has been followed ever since, and which has been usually incorporated in one of the rules reported as a matter of course at each convention by the committee on rules and order of business.

No change in the method of choosing the national committee was made in 1864 or 1868, but for reasons

[1] Jesse Macy, *Party Organization and Machinery*, 65, 68. The Democratic party had had one for nearly ten years, viz.: since 1848.

[2] See *supra,* pages 51, 52.

discussed elsewhere, [1] the committee was called "National Union Committee" or "National Executive Committee." [2]

In 1880, in addition to the usual rule prescribing the method of appointing members of the national committee, the committee was directed "within twelve months to prescribe a method or methods for the election of delegates to the Republican national convention to be held in 1884 and announce the same to the country and issue a call for that convention in conformity therewith."

In 1884 the membership of the national committee was restricted by an extraordinary amendment [3] to the usual rule, adopted by the convention providing that "No person should be a member of the Committee who was not eligible as a member to the electoral college," thus excluding from membership on the national committee any person holding a federal office under the Constitution of the United States.

In 1888, the usual rule relative to the formation of the national committee received the following addition:

The Republican National Committee is authorized and empowered to select an Executive Committee to consist of nine members who may or may not be members of the National Committee.

This has been substantially re-adopted at all suc-

[1] See *supra*, pages 88, 89.

[2] "The Second Birth of the Republican Party," W. A. Dunning, *American Historical Review*, XVI, 56 (Oct., 1910).

[3] The purpose of the amendment is described in the footnote to page 146, *supra*. This provision was never again adopted and the question has never again been raised in connection with the national committee.

ceeding conventions. Beginning in 1860, it had been customary for the national committee to form an executive committee from amongst its own membership, but this was the first time the practice received official sanction and the first time that permission was granted the national committee to form an executive committee from others than its own members.

A resolution was also adopted at the convention of 1884, as follows:

That in case of a vacancy occurring in the Republican National Committee, such vacancy may be filled by the State Central Committee of the State, Territory or District thus left unrepresented.

This has become the regular practice.

As we have seen, under the rule adopted in 1860 (and reported at each succeeding convention, with the additions and changes noted above), "usually on the second or third day after the adoption of the platform and before the nominations of the candidates, the permanent chairman of the national convention, declares the next order of business to be the calling of the roll of the States and Territories for the presentation of the names of persons chosen to serve on the national committee" for the next four years. Such is the rule, but the practice is otherwise, for the secretary of the convention usually has in advance a full report of the names of the members chosen from each State and Territory and when this report is read to the convention it is accepted as it stands, unless objections are made from the floor. Little, if any, control over the choice of the members of the national committee is therefore exercised by the national convention as such.

"This is left to each State and is frequently determined by a caucus among the party leaders in advance."

Perhaps there is no element of national party machinery which has developed along lines more unexpected than the national committee. Little did the chairman of the Pittsburg convention think when he appointed a "National Executive Committee" that he was making one of the most important precedents which that first Republican national convention set, and that he was establishing a party organ which would arrogate to itself at times almost unlimited powers and supreme control of the national party machinery.

Historically speaking, the committee has grown in consequence and power with the growth of the party. "As the party has become the regular and accepted organ of political expression, the national committee chosen in orderly manner and surrounded by all the sanctions of an established institution, intrenched in the habits and affections of a great people, has supplanted the irregular and self-appointed agencies of the earlier days and assumed prestige and authority,"[1] undreamed of at the time of its creation.

This development of the national committee in importance is well reflected in the official proceedings and contemporary records and magazines.

Of the first national committee appointed by the chairman of the informal Pittsburg convention in 1856, an examination of the contemporary records and official proceedings reveals almost nothing. It consisted of about twenty-two members with Edwin D. Morgan,

[1] J. Macy, *Party Organization and Machinery,* 65.

who subsequently became Governor of New York, as chairman. The convention having itself voted to hold a national nominating convention at Philadelphia and fixed the date and method of representation, there was nothing left for the national executive committee to do but to draw up the wording of the call and issue it, which as we have seen the committee did.[1] But four lines are devoted in the official proceedings of the convention to the work of this first national committee [2] and the contemporary press and magazines paid practically no attention to its doings.

The Philadelphia convention selected a national committee of twenty-five members. All that the *Official Proceedings*[3] tell us as to the operations of this committee is that it met at the Girard House in Philadelphia after the termination of the convention and chose Edwin D. Morgan, chairman, and N. B. Judd, secretary. Thanks to the resolution [4] of Judge Hoar of Massachusetts, the convention left the naming of the time and place for holding the next national convention, four years hence, to the national committee; and nothing being said about the method of representation, the national committee took it upon itself to determine that question.

As to the work of the national committe, whether it labored arduously to secure the election of Fremont, little, if anything, is known. The official proceedings

---

[1] See *supra,* page 37.

[2] *Official proceedings of the first three Republican National Conventions,* etc., p. 14.

[3] *Ibid.,* p. 42.

[4] See *supra,* page 51.

are entirely silent on this subject and contemporary magazines and newspapers contain practically nothing, save the names of the committee, together with a brief description of its personnel. It did, however, issue the call for the convention of 1860 and the chairman, Mr. Morgan, again called the convention together and named the temporary president, accounting for his action at the same time as follows: "Usage has made it my duty to take the preliminary steps to organize the convention." [1]

In the marvelous campaign which was waged for Lincoln's election, it is doubtful whether the national committee played any important part, as Lincoln had campaign managers[2] and a committee of his own.

The convention of 1860 selected a national committee of twenty-three members which issued the call for the convention of 1864. Owing to the exigencies of the times, in addition to fixing the date and place for holding the convention, it assumed the responsibility of suppressing the party name. [3] The official proceedings of the convention give us no information as to what the national committee or its chairman did. Beyond a list of the names attached to the official call, no mention is made of the committee or its personnel, save the statement that Mr. Morgan as chairman called the convention to order and in the behalf of the national committee proposed a temporary president of the

[1] *Official proceedings of the first three Republican National Conventions,* etc., p. 84.

[2] See *supra,* page 75.

[3] See *supra,* pages 88, 89.

convention and a committee of two to escort him to the chair. Temporary secretaries were not at this time named by the national committee, but were selected upon motion of a regular delegate.

At a meeting held in Chicago, May 18, 1860, the national committee chosen at this convention, organized by selecting Hon. Edwin D. Morgan of New York as chairman and George F. Fogg of New Hampshire, as secretary. Subsequently, an executive committee was chosen by the committee, consisting of seven of its members. This was the first executive committee of the national committee of which we have any record and it became the fixed practice for the national committee to organize by forming an executive committee from its own members. This custom, as we have seen, received official sanction in 1888, after which time also, many of the members of the executive committee were chosen outside of the national committee.

The official proceedings of 1864 give a list of the members selected for the new national committee for the next four years and make no further mention of the committee, its officers and doings. The committee selected as its headquarters the City of Chicago, and chose Henry J. Raymond of New York as its chairman and John D. De Frees as secretary. The selection of Mr. Raymond [1] was made not with a view of having a campaign manager and friend of the presidential candidate at the committee's head, as we shall see subsequently became the custom, but to honor a representa-

---

[1] Editor of the New York *Times;* the platforms of 1856 and 1864 were the work of Mr. Raymond. His services in the political campaign of 1864 contributed greatly to the success of the Republican party (Maverick, *Raymond and New York Journalism,* 168).

tive of the party actively associated with the national organization from its birth. Mr. Raymond's resignation prior to the convention 1868 necessitated the selection of a new chairman and the committee then elected Marcus L. Ward of New Jersey and he accordingly signed the call and opened the proceedings of that gathering.

The proceedings of the national convention of 1868 contain a list of the members selected for the next national committee, which had now grown to the number of forty-two. Just before the convention adjourned, the president announced that the committee would meet at eight-thirty that evening at the Tremont House in Chicago to organize. The proceedings further enlighten us as to the method of this organization, which was as follows. William Claflin was chosen chairman, and William E. Chandler, secretary. Four headquarters were established for the national committee and four separate executive committees appointed. The so-called central executive committee, with headquarters at New York City, was composed of the chairman, Mr. Claflin, and six members, among whom were Horace Greeley and Marsh Giddings. In addition there was an executive committee for the West with headquarters at Chicago and one for the South, with headquarters at Atlanta, Georgia, each consisting of three members. There was also an executive committee for the Pacific Coast, with headquarters at San Francisco, California, consisting of two members.

The national committee chosen by the convention of 1872, consisting of forty-seven men, organized by the election of Governor Edwin D. Morgan as chairman, and William E. Chandler as secretary, and formed an executive committee of sixteen of its members, with the headquarters of the committee at the Fifth Avenue Hotel, New York City.

The selection of Mr. Claflin in 1868 and of Mr. Morgan in 1872 was made after consultation with General Grant and the practice of consulting the presidential candidate as to whom the committee should select as its chairman may be said to date from that time; but in neither case was the selection made with a view of having a campaign manager or special friend of the presidential candidate or a man of wealth or influence. The selection was based on being a worthy representative of the national party.

Beginning with the national convention of 1872, the official proceedings take notice of a "Republican Congressional Committee" [1] and likewise print a full record of the chairmen and secretaries of the Republican State committees, at that time thirty-seven in number. The proceedings of nearly all succeeding conventions record the full list of members of the Republican national committee for the specific year and its organization and treat similarly of the Republican congressional committee and the several State com-

In 1876, the national committee at a meeting held after the convention adjourned elected Zachariah Chandler as chairman and William E. Chandler as secretary and also selected an executive committee of eighteen members which latter had a chairman and secretary of its own. The committee established two headquarters, the Eastern one at New York City, and the Western at Chicago.[2]

[1] See *infra.*

[2] Frequently the location of headquarters has been fixed with a

Unlike the national committee chairmen to whom we have hitherto referred, "Zack and Bill Chandler" were chosen for their ability as political compaigners and they "made the fight in '76". They were chosen by the committee after careful consultation with the presidential candidate and it was directly through Zachariah Chandler's efforts in securing the electoral votes of Louisiana, Florida and South Carolina, that Hayes was elected.

After President Hayes' election William Chandler resigned and Col. T. B. Keogh was elected secretary. Zachariah Chandler died before the convention of 1880, and the call for that year was accordingly signed by Mr. J. D. Cameron, whom the committee selected to succeed Mr. Chandler.

At the convention of 1880, Mr. Cameron proposed in addition to the names of a temporary chairman and committee of two, to escort him to the chair, also, the names for the other temporary officers of the convention, to wit, secretaries, reading clerks and a stenographer. Until that date, the minor officers of the convention had been nominated from the floor or otherwise chosen by the comvention.

The national committee of 1880 organized in considerable detail. Governor Marshall Jewell was General Garfield's choice for chairman. John A. Martin

view to the strategic value of having centres of the campaign near or in doubtful States, as for instance, in 1896, when the Republican national committee selected Chicago as the point from which the then militant forces in the field were to be controlled, as it did also in 1900 when one of its headquarters was located in New York and the other in Chicago.

was chosen secretary, and Washington was selected as the headquarters of the committee.

The committee elected Governor Jewell at the direct suggestion of General Garfield for whom he managed the campaign with great ability and energy.[1] Governor Jewell's death prior to the convention of 1884 necessitated a new choice by the committee and D. M. Sabin was chosen and issued the call for that convention.

At length in 1884, the compiler of the proceedings of the Republican national convention begins to include in his record some detail as to the actions and industries of the previous national committee and the various sub-committees. According to his account, at a meeting of the national committee held in the City of Washington on the 12th day of December, 1883, a sub-committee was chosen, consisting of seven members and charged with the duty of visiting Chicago, appointing a local committee of arrangements and taking charge of the preparations for the convention. The sub-committee held a meeting at the Grand Pacific Hotel, Chicago, on Saturday, March 22d, 1884, and appointed a local committee of arrangements, consisting of nineteen members, none of whom were members of the national committee, but all prominent citizens of the State of Illinois.

A finance committee of some two dozen members was also appointed, who provided means for preparing a proper hall in the Exposition Building, and defraying the other necessary expenses of the convention. This committee made a vigorous canvass of the city and speedily raised a fund sufficient to cover the expenses

[1] Tweedy, *History of Republican National Conventions,* 202, 203.

of the convention. Sub-committees to take charge of necessary details, such as transportation, hotels, press, printing, official reporting and official publication, telegraphy, music, decoration, employees, auditing, state headquarters and hall were appointed by the chairman of the local committee of arrangements, and, on recommendation of this local committee, the national sub-committee appointed Col. James A. Sexton, sergeant-at-arms, and designated certain official reporters to do the reporting of the convention.

The local organization thus perfected carried forward the preparations with complete success, including even the fitting up of rooms for the use of the Associated press, several telegraph companies and the reporters of the daily press. The national committee met in Chicago a few days before the day set for the meeting of the convention, and the hall, in which the convention was to meet, was then turned over to them by the local committee of arrangements, at which time the national committee adopted a resolution of thanks to the local committee on arrangement and finance.

The national committee, chosen by the convention of 1884 to conduct the campaign of that year and to call the convention of 1888, consisted of forty-seven delegates and organized by the selection of B. F. Jones as chairman, Samuel Fessenden, as secretary and John L. Ward as treasurer and placed its headquarters at Number 242 Fifth Avenue, New York City.

In this year also the wishes of the presidential nominee were consulted and the election of Mr. Jones by the committee was at the earnest request of Mr. Blaine.[1]

---

[1] The campaign fund at the disposal of the national committee in

Since the organization of the first regular Republican national convention, it has been the prerogative and duty of the national committee, as we have seen, to choose the time and place at which the next national convention was to be held. Owing to the eager desire, of the various large cities of the country, to secure the honor of having the convention held within their limits, and the inducements offered by each city there has sometimes been a spirited contest on the question in the national committee.

In December of 1887, the national committee held a meeting at its Washington headquarters at which delegates from various cities attended to urge the merits of their respective homes upon the national committee, to influence its choice of a place for holding the next national convention. Mayor Roche of Chicago and Senators Cullom and Farwell of Illinois, together with a large delegation from that State, presented the merits of Chicago with such earnestness that the committee selected that City. The duty of taking charge of the preparation for the convention was again intrusted to a sub-committee composed of nine members of the national committee with the chairman and secretary of the national committee as *ex-officio* members. This sub-committee chose its own chairman and secretary and, meeting in February, 1888, at the Grand Pacific Hotel in Chicago, appointed committees of citizens to take charge of arrangements and look after details locally. An executive and finance committee was se-

that year was only about $400,000, a large part of which Mr. Blaine himself contributed. Mr. Jones was one of the wealthy Pittsburg iron-masters.

lected, as well as committees on hotels, printing, press, transportation, employees, music, decorations, State headquarters, hall, telegraph, auditing, official reporting, and publication. The sub-committee, on the recommendation of the executive and finance committee, appointed a sergeant-at-arms. Five days before the time of meeting of the convention, the Auditorium Building, with a seating capacity of 8,550 persons was turned over by the local committee to the sub-committee and by them to the regular national committee, and appropriate resolutions of thanks were passed.

Students of politics have been greatly interested in endeavoring to obtain an adequate explanation of the fact that although Senator Matthew S. Quay of Pennsylvania is always referred to as the chairman of the Republican national committee (selected by the convention of 1888) that conducted the campaign which resulted in the election of President Harrison, yet no official record of any of Mr. Quay's actions as chairman is apparently in existence.

The call for the convention of 1892, issued by the national committee in that year is signed by James S. Clarkson as chairman, without any mention of or reference to Mr. Quay.

Little, however, is disclosed of the inner workings of a Republican national committee and it was to obtain enlightenment upon the apparent inconsistency above mentioned, that the writer communicated with Senator Boies Penrose of Pennsylvania, who was a close friend of the late Matthew S. Quay.

Senator Penrose kindly referred the writer to Mr. James S. Clarkson, at present residing in this city, and through the courtesy of Mr. E. W. Bloomingdale an interview was had with the former First Assistant Postmaster General.

Mr. Clarkson's explanation was: Mr. Harrison was nominated in the national convention of 1888 by the "swinging" to him of the so-called "Old Blaine Crowd" or progressive element of that time.   Mr. Clarkson was a member of the "Old Blaine Crowd" and had for many years been a close personal friend of General Harrison.

After receiving the nomination, General Harrison sent for Mr. Clarkson and requested him to accept the chairmanship of the national committee.   Mr. Clarkson, however, advised General Harrison that the "Old Grant Crowd" or "Stalwarts," led by Senator Conkling and other supporters of General Grant, should be encouraged and placated and suggested that the interests of General Harrison would be best served if the chairman were selected from the other element, and that Mr. Quay, who was a member of the "Old Guard," and also of the national committee, and who had been very prominent in Pennsylvania, would be an excellent choice.

General Harrison acquiesced and thereupon Mr. Clarkson communicated with Mr. Charles Emory Smith of Philadelphia, who represented the anti-Quay element in Pennsylvania, as to whether any objection would be raised were such a selection made, and being advised in the negative Mr. Quay was asked to accept the position of chairman of the national committee, which he did.

In July the committee's headquarters were established in New York, and as Mr. Quay (whom Mr. Clarkson regards as the greatest political general this country has ever had) was unable to come to New York until September, the office of vice-chairman was created to enable Mr. Clarkson to perform the active duties of chairmanship [1] during Mr. Quay's absence.

After General Harrison's election, differences arose between the President and Mr. Quay because of the latter's dissatisfaction with the recognition which the President had accorded him and the national committee.

President Harrison desired Mr. Quay's retirement from the chairmanship but through the intervention of Mr. Clarkson matters were smoothed over.

The breach between the President and Mr. Quay widened because of the great reluctance with which the President made the appointment of Mr. John Wanamaker as Postmaster General of the United States under the recommendation and strenuous insistence of Mr. Quay.

In 1891 the President sent for Mr. Clarkson upon his return from abroad and again urged that the resignation of Mr. Quay should be procured. Mr. Clarkson thought that the time had arrived when the national committee ought to listen to the wishes of the President and consented to act as an intermediary, particularly as Mr. Quay was desirous of resigning

[1] The extensive campaign work, especially that part which is of a literary character began under the chairmanship of Mr. Quay and Mr. Clarkson and the practice was extended of distributing literature in various foreign tongues, adapted to the peculiar social position and religious persuasion of the different classes of voters,—a practice which has ever since prevailed and the details of which have been greatly elaborated and enlarged. For its services in this regard the Committee received a vote of thanks at the Convention of 1892. *Official Proceedings, etc., 1892*, p. 122.

because of the conflict between his senatorial duties and his activities as national committee chairman.

At the meeting of the national committee in 1891, where the President was represented by Mr. Charles Foster of Ohio, then Secretary of the Treasury, Mr. Quay resigned and the wishes of the President were fulfilled.

Mr. Clarkson who, up to this time had been vice-chairman, thereupon assumed the position of chairman, and Mr. Hobart, who later became Vice-President of the United States, took the office of vice-chairman. Mr. J. Sloat Fassett remained as secretary of the committee, and Mr. Barber of Pennsylvania became treasurer.

Accordingly the call issued in January, 1892 bore Mr. Clarkson's signature as chairman of the national committee and, by virtue of that office, he called the national convention of that year to order.

It should also be noted that in 1888, pursuant to the authority given to the committee by the national convention in that year,[1] the committee selected an executive committee of nine members, some of whom were members of the national committee and the rest prominent politicians from different localities in the Union.

Headquarters were open for the committee at the Plaza Hotel, New York, and at the Arlington Hotel in the City of Washington. On the 21st of November, 1891, a public hearing was held at the Washington headquarters of the committee and the claims of several cities presented to the committee, and their availability urged for holding the next national con-

[1] See *supra*.

vention. Seven ballots were taken by the committee and the claims of nearly a dozen cities presented,[1] the final ballot resulting in favor of Minneapolis, which was represented by a delegation of nearly a hundred of the prominent men of the Northwest. A fund of $50,000 was guaranteed to the national committee on condition that the convention be held in that city. The perfection of the preliminary arrangements was intrusted to the executive committee of the national committee to perfect, and this committee authorized Chairman Clarkson to appoint a sub-committee to take entire charge of all arrangements necessary to the holding of the convention. The chairman appointed such a committee, consisting of eight members with himself and the secretary as *ex-officio* members and likewise selected a sergeant-at-arms to whom was intrusted the duty of superintending the printing of tickets and the organization of the necessary force of assistant sergeant-at-arms, ushers and pages to seat the people and to maintain order during the sessions of the convention. The sub-committee appointed a local citizens' executive committee as well as the usual specific local committees which had been employed in former years, adding this time a committee on State headquarters and a ladies' reception committee. The fifty thousand dollar guarantee fund was nearly doubled and a twelve story office building was secured for the use of the press alone.

Thomas H. Carter of Montana, who was not a member of the original national committee was chosen as

[1] *Proceedings of the 10th Republican National Convention, held in the City of Minneapolis, Minnesota, June 7th, 8th, 9th and 10th, 1892,* p. 6.

the chairman of the Republican national committee appointed by the convention of 1892, and Joseph H. Manley was chosen secretary. The selection of Mr. Carter was likewise made at the suggestion of General Harrison.

The national committee chosen at the convention of 1896 marks a new era. The committee organized by the formation of an executive committee of twenty members, (eleven of whom, including the chairman of the national committee, occupied headquarters of the Auditorium Hotel, Chicago, and nine of whom had headquarters in the Metropolitan Life Building, New York City), and by chosing Marcus A. Hanna of Ohio, as chairman, and Charles Dick of Ohio, as secretary. Cornelius N. Bliss of New York was chosen treasurer, and there was also appointed a sub-treasurer and a member of the executive committee in charge of the bureau of speakers and another in charge of literary and press matters.[1] None of these men, including the chairman himself, were members of the original national committee appointed by the convention of 1892, but they formed a part of the national committee, under the resolution adopted in 1888, previously referred to.

Mr. Hanna had managed Major McKinley's canvass for the nomination with headquarters at Cleveland, Ohio, for months prior to the convention of 1886 with signal ability and was generally recognized as the right man to take charge of the campaign for his elec-

---

[1] Two hundred and seventy-eight different newspapers from thirty-eight different States had representatives at the national convention of 1896.

tion. His selection by Mr. McKinley was accordingly
ratified by the vote of the committee.

This national committee of 1896, its chairman,
officers, general method of organization and powers,
became the prototype of all succeeding national committees, with this exception that in 1900 and subsequent years the national committee has selected an
advisory committee as an auxiliary to itself. This
advisory committee is composed of Senators and members of the Federal Cabinet at Washington, as well
as other prominent politicians and statesmen [1] and
usually numbers from thirty to fifty members. In
1900, the national committee had risen to such prominence that the official proceedings contain not merely
a perfunctory list of its members and officers, but likewise a detailed statement of its several headquarters,
the delegates and officers attached to each, as well as
a full list of the advisory committee, containing among
others the names of Senators Platt, Depew and Aldrich.
The pictures of the chairman, Mr. Hanna, and of the
chairman of the sub-committee on arrangements, Mr.
Hanley, are also printed in the proceedings, and in
1904 the photographs of the chairman for that year,
Mr. Cortelyou, as well as those of other prominent
officers of the national committee for that year and
preceding years are reproduced.

[1] In 1904, Chairman Cortelyou had a large advisory committee composed of skilled politicians from all sections. They never met as a
body but communicated with the chairman by letter or in person,
telling him of the progress of the fight in their several States. Speaker
Cannon and Senator Frye, most especially represented the House and
the Senate on the advisory committee. In addition there were a dozen
or more Representatives and Senators besides many other prominent
citizens including Federal and State officials.

Magazines and newspapers pay a similarly increased attention to the national committee and its officers, particularly its chairman and treasurer, and beginning with 1896, the working of the national committee and the character and personality of the chairman of the national committee are the subject of much attention.[1]

Thus it would appear that the chairman though nominally chosen by the committee has in reality since 1868 been selected by the presidential candidate. In fact it has been customary for the Republican nominee for the past forty years to select his own campaign manager and for the national committee to then elect his choice to its chairmanship whether he be a member of the original national committee or not. This has been due to a large extent to the natural connection and identity of interest between the President's campaign manager and the chairman of the national party committee; so that unless the President's selection were peculiarly distasteful to the majority of the committee they would naturally ratify his choice.

Prior to 1868 it may be noticed the national committee chairman played little or no part as a campaign manager. From 1868 to 1880 the committee's so-called choice combined close attachment to the presidential nominee with representation of the national party but

---

[1] "George B. Cortelyou and the Republican Campaign," *Review of Reviews*, XXX, 294-8.

"The Management of the Taft Campaign," *Review of Reviews*, XXXVIII, 432-8.

"Chairman Frank H. Hitchcock," *Review of Reviews*, XXXVIII, 438-42.

"How the Republican National Committee Works for Votes," *Review of Reviews*, XXII, 549-55.

since the Blaine campaign of 1884 while in some years both qualifications may have been present the choice was primarily for an active experienced campaign manager rather than a particular representative of the national party. In some years in fact the committee has been divided and there was talk of replacing the presidential candidate's choice after election by a more representative man of the party but this has never been done.

Once chosen by the presidential nominee the chairman has absolute control of the entire campaign and "wields the power of a commander-in-chief in regard to everybody."

Every national committee is a rule to itself obeying neither rule nor precedent and no official records of its acts are preserved.

The origin and development of the part which the national committee plays in issuing the call for the convention and in forming the preliminary organization of that gathering have been previously detailed.

When the national convention has been organized, the authority of the national committee is ended, though the chairman retains his office until the new national committee, chosen for the ensuing four years by the delegates at the convention has been organized.

While much is known concerning the work[1] which the Republican national committees have performed

---

[1] "The Republican National Committee; How it works for votes," *Review of Reviews*, XXII, 529. It was estimated that the Republican committee in 1896 sent out about 20,000 express packages, 5,000 freight packages and probably half a million packages by mail. Nearly a hundred different documents and a dozen or more posters were put out in 1900. 80,000,000 copies of them at a cost of $164,000,

during the presidential campaigns which have occurred during the past thirty years, little information as to their operations throughout the three intervening years is to be found. The duties of that period are however numerous and important. " 'To promote the Democratic cause' was one of the labors assigned to its committee by the Democratic convention of 1848, and this may be taken as a comprehensive statement of the work of a national committee. A common cause of party weakness and failure is the rise of misunderstandings, division and local faction within the party. The committee, representing in theory the whole party constituency of the country, is in a position to resist the development of faction and to exercise powerful influence in correcting misunderstandings and healing dissensions. Along such lines, its practical usefulness may be almost unlimited and much of its time during the years of comparative inaction is devoted to the labor of harmonizing elements, possibly discordant." [1]   It may also actively assist in discovering and determining the will of the party and of the country.

For the very reason that the committee does not authoritatively conduct the elections held during the

and 3,000,000 campaign buttons of different sorts were sent out. As soon as the issues of the campaign are pretty well settled, the national committee prints and distributes a campaign text book which usually contains the platform, notification and acceptance speeches, biographical sketches of the candidates, statistics on business, tariff, trusts, money and other economic issues, addresses by prominent leaders and the most cogent arguments which the party can advance in defense of its position.

In 1896 the cost of this branch of the work was something over $700,000, and in 1900,—the text book being a closely printed well bound volume of 456 pages,—it came close to a million dollars.

[1] J. Macy, *Party Organization and Machinery,* 68, 69.

three years, intervening between the presidential campaigns, it is enabled all the more effectively to obtain full and accurate information as to the temper of the people all over the Union and, observing the course of public events and the development of national issues, it is "prepared to sum up the results for the benefit of the party in the conflict at the end of that period." [1]

The history of the Republican party furnishes numerous illustrations of this. Thus in December 1859 the call issued by the national committee for the convention of 1860 invited "the Republican electors of the several States, the members of the people's party of Pennsylvania, and the opposition party of New Jersey, and all others who are willing to co-operate with them in support of the candidates who shall be nominated." It was the national committee that decided whom to invite to the convention, and whose members assumed "the responsibility of designating" the people's party of Pennsylvania and the opposition party of New Jersey suitable component parts of that contention." [2]

In calling the convention, the national committee formulated in much detail what it regarded as the precise issues of the hour; such as, the right of Congress to prohibit the extension of slavery in the Territories, and the immediate admission of Kansas as a free State. Four years later the committee assumed the responsibility of suppressing the party name and neither in the call nor in any official report of the proceedings of the convention which followed, does the

[1] *Ibid.,* 69, 70.
[2] *Ibid.,* 70.

name Republican anywhere appear. It describes itself as "The undersigned, who by original appointment or by subsequent designation to fill vacancies,
constitute the Executive Committee created by the
National Convention held at Chicago on May 16th,
1860." Not a single reference is made to any opposing
party and all qualified voters, "who desire the unconditional maintenance of the Union, the supremacy of the
Constitution, and the complete suppression of the existing rebellion with the cause thereof, by vigorous war
and all apt and efficient means," are invited to send
delegates to the convention.[1]

The position of the Republican national committee
after 1860 "was a peculiarly delicate and responsible
one. As soon as the war had become serious, the ob-
noxious partisan name was dropped, as if by common
consent. All citizens, regardless of party, were called
upon to support the government and there was a
prompt and hearty response." [2]

"When the time for the meeting of the Republican
convention was approaching in 1864, the national
committee waited for two months after the usual date
for the holding of a non-partizan "Union Convention,"
assuming the responsibility of giving an entirely new
name to their party." [3] The national committee appointed by the "Union Convention" took the liberty of
restoring the Republican name in issuing the call for the
convention of 1868, adding the word Republican to the
previous title.[4]

[1] J. Macy, *Party Organization and Machinery*, 71.
[2] *Ibid.*, 72.
[3] J. Macy, *Party Organization and Machinery*, 72.
[4] *Official Proceedings, etc., 1876*, p. 233.

Again in 1876 we find Governor Morgan as chairman of the national committee suggesting what the committee regarded as issues on which the convention should take a definite stand and on which it should "put planks in the platform."

The quiet and almost unnoticed extension of political power by the Republican national committee during the past forty years has been truly remarkable. This simple agency of party activity of little more than a generation ago has silently assumed functions and privileges undreamed of at the time of its creation. It aims to-day to dictate to the very party which created it, to control conventions, prescribe candidates, distribute party rewards and to consolidate and perpetuate the power which has fallen into its hands. But its rise to power has been slow and gradual. Its early function, the only one described in histories of parties was very modest.

The change began in 1884 when Senator Gorman was chairman of the Democratic national committee. Cleveland's victory involved the re-organization of the whole Federal administration and office-holding body and Mr. Gorman, who had been in active control of the Democratic machine for the preceding five months, was called upon to sift the claims to political favor of thousands of Democrats unknown to the President elect. This new activity came to him not by virtue of his position as United States Senator but as national committee chairman. He became the leader in distributing patronage and to a great extent in determining party policy.

Matthew S. Quay, whose wonderful political generalship had contributed in so great a degree to Harrison's election in 1888, greatly enlarged the prerogatives and powers of the office he held,[1] which reached their culmination in Senator Marcus A. Hanna in 1896. He, more than any other party chairman before him, influenced the distribution of party patronage and kept a firm hand at all times on the levers of the national machine.

Accountable to no one and having a campaign fund of millions to distribute, the national committee chairman's power is to-day almost unlimited. He alone is fully cognizant of the express or tacit party obligations which have gone with the collection of this fund and becomes thus, as it were, a "repository of secret liens upon party action and the one mysterious agent by means of whom they are made good."

[1] *Proceedings of the Pennsylvania Legislature to commemorate the public services of Matthew S. Quay, March 22nd, 1905,* page 23.

The Republican Congressional Campaign Committee.

Further developing and centralizing the national party organization, there was formed shortly after the close of the Civil War, alongside of the national committee, another central committee at Washington—the congressional campaign committee—for the purpose of directing congressional campaigns. This committee always works in co-operation with the national committee, though entirely independent of it.

The members of the Republican congressional committee are appointed to the number of one for each State by the Republican Senators and Representatives of all the States meeting in joint caucus which is called by petition of party members in each House. At this meeting the Republican members from each State and Territory designate one of their number to serve on the committee. If there is but one party member in Congress from any State or Territory, that one becomes a member of the committee. If the State or Territory has no Republican Representative in Congress, it has no representation on the Republican congressional committee. There is no rule as to whether any of the members of the committee shall be Senators, though, as a matter of fact, some Senators are always chosen. The great majority are however from the Lower House.[1] After a new House of Representatives has been elected the congressional committee is reorganized, the former committee expiring with the Congress which created it.

[1] J. Macy, *Party Organization and Machinery,* 91.

"The origin of the congressional committee belongs to a time of sharp conflict [1] between the executive and legislative branches of the government.[2] In the national convention of the Republican party which nominated Lincoln and Johnson in 1864, the name Union was for reasons previously detailed [3] substituted for Republican. That body included and represented many supporters of the Lincoln administration who were not Republicans and it was on account of the Union Democrats in the convention that Mr. Johnson's name was placed upon the ticket.[4] When Johnson became President the great body of the Republicans in Congress were driven into opposition and the support of the Executive came mainly from the Democrats. It is unnecessary to give the details of the famous conflict that followed, out of which came a number of changes [5] in

[1] The events which occurred during the administration of Andrew Johnson furnished the most conspicuous instance in our history of the rivalry of leadership between Congress and the Executive.

[2] J. Macy, *Party Organization and Machinery,* 30, 87.

[3] See *supra,* pages 88, *et seq.*

[4] Andrew Johnson, a Southern man, had always been a Democrat, but along with many other Democrats, he was a strong Unionist and had been devoted to the support of the first Lincoln administration. In recognition of this branch of the Union party, the name of Johnson was placed upon the ticket and by the death of Lincoln a man who had never borne the Republican party name became President.

[5] "Another sequence to the events of Johnson's term, though one that could not be so readily proven to have grown out of the contest between the two departments of the government, is that since that time, members of Congress have had a larger proportionate share in the distribution of party patronage." At that time Congress passed laws restraining the President in the matter of appointments. "Though these laws were afterwards repealed, the members of the two Houses have nevertheless retained a considerable part of the patronage which

party organization and party leadership. Since the Republican party was left without a presidential leader, the two Houses of Congress looked about them for an efficient substitute. This was the situation when the time approached for the election of a new Congress in 1866. The President having control of the public patronage was using it to strengthen his administration. The national party committee closely identified as it was with the Executive was an unsatisfactory agency for the use of the Republicans in Congress. In this emergency, that the party might not suffer in the congressional elections of 1866, the Republican members of the two Houses agreed upon the appointment of a national committee of their own to take charge of the elections in the several States. They "organized and conducted a campaign and secured a representation in Congress strong enough to enable them to overcome the President's veto."[1]

The new central party organ[2] called the congressional campaign committee, in watching the electoral situation in the congressional districts penetrated more deeply and more continuously into local political life than could have been done by the permanent committee of the national convention which made its appearance on the eve of and principally in view of the presidential election.

law and earlier usage had given to the President." (J. Macy, *Party Organization and Machinery*, 32.)

[1] J. Macy, *Party Organization and Machinery*, 87-88.

[2] A few years after the formation of the first Republican congressional committee, the Democratic party followed the Republican example, but differed somewhat in method of organization from the Republican model.

In the official proceedings of the convention of 1872 for the first time mention is made, of the existence of a Republican congressional committee and, under the heading of "Union Republican Congressional Committee," a list of the thirty-eight members of Congress constituting the committee of that year together with the respective States which they represented, is given. The record also shows that an executive committee of eleven members of the congressional committee was formed of whom Zachariah Chandler was chairman, James M. Edmunds, secretary, and H. D. Clark, treasurer, and that the headquarters of the committee were located at Washington, D. C.

A more detailed organization of the Republican congressional committee is revealed in the official proceedings of the convention of 1876. The committee consisted of thirty-five members, and this time we find that three committees were appointed: an executive committee of nine members, of which Simon Cameron

In the organization of the Democratic congressional committee the following differences from the Republican model should be noted, viz.: In the first place, the members of the committee instead of being chosen at a joint caucus of the two Houses are appointed at separate caucuses of the Houses. There is also a definite rule respecting the representation from each House. The Senate has nine members on the committee appointed by the senatorial caucus and in addition to these, each State and Territory which has representatives in the lower House has a member from that House on the committee. If it happens that any State or Territory has no party member of the House of Representatives, then some prominent Democrat in the State or Territory is chosen to serve on the committee. The Democratic method creates a much larger committee than does the Republican method. In 1903, the Democratic committee numbered 59; the Republican, 34. An interesting discussion of this difference in the organization of the congressional committees of the two great parties is found in J. Macy, *Party Organization and Machinery*, 92.

was chairman and which numbered among its members John A. Logan and Thomas C. Platt; a committee of three on finance, and a committee of three on printing. In addition to the chairman there was a secretary, treasurer and chief clerk for the committee, the latter not being a member of the committee. The headquarters were located at 1006-F Street N. W., Washington, D. C.

Variations are noticeable in the comparative influence and importance of the Republican congressional committee at different periods during the past forty years of its existence.

The official proceedings of the national conventions for the years 1880, 1884, 1888 and 1892 contain no reference of any kind to the existence of a congressional committee, doubtless due to the fact that in 1880 (though the committee was active in the campaign of that year) a breach arose between the national committee and the congressional committee At that time many persons advised the abandonment of the double national party committee system and for some twelve years thereafter the activities of the Republican congressional committee almost ceased, but in 1894 it emerged [1] once more and assumed its duties particularly in the congressional field, so that we find the Republican congressional committee and its officers and organization once more chronicled in detail in the official proceedings of the convention of 1896. Its organization at this time consisted of a chairman, vice-chairman, secretary, assistant-secretary and treasurer and also an executive committee of six members among

[1] J. Macy, *Party Organization and Machinery,* 92.

whom appeared such prominent men as Joseph G. Cannon and James S. Sherman. The committee proper consisted of forty-one members and its headquarters were as usual at Washington, D. C.

The official proceedings of all subsequent Republican national conventions refer to the organization of the Republican congressional committee, giving in detail its officers, members and executive committee together with the States, Territories and dependencies represented. The one change to which reference should be made is, that in 1904 the headquarters of the committee were located at 1135 Broadway, New York City.

It is only occasionally that we gain any glimpses into the inner operations of the Republican congressional committee and we are fortunate in having this interesting account from the biography of Zachariah Chandler, [1] published by the Detroit *Post and Tribune*, in 1880:

In the general elections of 1870 and 1872, Mr. Chandler was exceedingly active, devoting much time to organization and to the general distribution of political literature. The latter branch of party effort had become the special province of the Republican Congressional Committee. For more than twenty years (this was in 1880) there have been two distinct executive organizations within the Republican party, independent of each other, but always working in harmony, namely: The National Committee and the Congressional Committee. The latter is composed of a representative in Congress from each State chosen by the Republican members of the respective delegations. No man can serve upon the committee unless he holds a seat in Congress, and States which have no Republican Congressman are unrepresented in

[1] *Zachariah Chandler*, 312, 313.

its membership. Mr. Chandler and Mr. James W. Edmunds were the founders of the Congressional Committee as a practical and influential working body; their plans and efforts first made it a power in American politics * * * The special objects which it aimed to accomplish were the securing of a uniform treatment of political topics by newspapers and speakers throughout the country and the circulation of instructive and timely documents. During the reconstruction era it also devoted much attention to the work of Republican organization in the South where special efforts were necessary to form into effective voting masses the emancipated slaves. But the great aim of the committee was the circulation of political literature. This end it sought to reach by two methods; first by the publication and mailing to individuals and to local committees in all parts of the country of such congressional speeches as dealt effectively with the current political situation; second, by furnishing the Republican Press, through the medium of weekly sheets of carefully prepared matter, with accurate information as to the facts underlying existing issues and suggestions as to their best treatment before the people. Obviously this work could be done best in Washington. * * * Hence it was deemed wise to establish a system of guidance, from that point, of the public discussions of each national campaign so that increased intelligence, cohesion and efficiency could be given to the general attack on the enemy.

In the beginning, then, the congressional committee was a party instrumentality adopted to meet an emergency only, "but it was not long before it had so commended itself to the party leaders as to be accepted and made a permanent part of the organization," and has ever since remained in active service long after the passing away of the special exigency which gave it birth. It has become an accepted organ of both parties because of the conviction that since Congress has its distinct place in party leadership and since its membership is renewed by elections occurring every other year, it has need of its own special party agency.

The national convention and the national committee though nominally and truly representing the entire party are in respect to their peculiar duties more specifically connected with the Executive. "That committee is indeed in a way the special agent of the presidential candidate appointed to secure his election and identified with his interests; but members of Congress, even of the same political connection, have duties and interests quite distinct from those of the Executive and the national congressional committee is an institutional recognition of this patent and significant fact. It not infrequently happens that serious differences arise between the President and his party in Congress, and it is highly important that these dissensions should not be allowed to mar the party unity in the voting constituency. Conceding the President's prior claim upon the original national committee, Congress can place full confidence in a committee of its own members connecting it directly with the local organizations in each congressional district." [1]

The usefulness of the congressional committee is especially demonstrated in the election campaigns occurring in the "off years," that is to say, those years in which the congressional elections occur. Members of the national committee may also, as individuals, take an active part in these elections, but the committee does not

[1] J. Macy, *Party Organization & Machinery,* 88.

organize and take charge of the campaign as in presidential years. This is now the province of the congressional committee, whose members have been "selected
by their colleagues for their political astuteness in con
ducting campaigns." It prepares and issues a campaign text book and other "political literature" and
assists doubtful districts by supplying speakers and
funds for campaign purposes. The committee does not
put forth a formal platform but assumes that the declaration of principles promulgated by the last preceding national convention is in force so far as it is applicable to the existing conditions. When new issues
have arisen, as in the case of the war with Spain in
1898, the attitude of the party toward those questions
will find expression in the campaign literature prepared by its congressional committee.[1]

The congressional committee also distributes documents, chiefly Republican congressional speeches and
public reports under congressional franks. Before the
campaign is ended, many millions of these, weighing
tons, have been sent out from its distributing office in
Washington. The congressional literature appeals especially to the country voter. The literary bureau of
the national committee does not trench upon the distributing work of the congressional committee. "It
seeks to make its news service attractive, to entertain
while it educates. Statistics that talk, cartoons and
striking posters are some of its best methods."

In congressional years, the congressional committee
pays little heed to national policy, platforms or pro-

[1] J. Macy, *Party Organization and Machinery*, 89.

grams and simply endeavors to insure the success at the congressional elections of the candidates who bear the party label whatever their political complexion. It divides all the congressional districts into three categories: the good, the hopeless and the doubtful; almost neglecting the first two groups, it directs all its efforts toward the districts of the last group.[1] In the interval between the elections, it follows the fortunes of the party in the districts attentively, ascertaining the vote of each succeeding election by counties and inquiring into the causes if it notes a fall in the number of votes polled by the candidate of the party. The committee likewise interposes to reconcile opposing factions and is in close touch with all the county committees in the Union, which point out to it the special steps necessary to strengthen the party in their several congressional districts and in general look to the congressional committee for advice and assistance.[2]

There are no fixed rules governing the relations of the two national party committees to each other. They must of course work in harmony [3] for the triumph of

[1] In this respect it differs materially from the Democratic congressional committee which seeks to add strength to the party in all sections alike. For the reason of this difference, see J. Macy, *Party Organization and Machinery*, 92.

[2] Campaign funds are supplied to the congressional committee, but these donations are much smaller than the ones received by the national committee. In the congressional campaign of 1908-9 varying estimates place it from $125,000 to $750,000. (New York *Times*, January 12th, 1909.)

[3] Evidence of the co-operation of the national and congressional committees was furnished in the campaign of 1904 in which James A. Tawney who acted as chief of the speakers' bureau of the national

the party and in presidential years the congressional committee occupies a relatively subordinate position. On the opening of the presidential campaign, it places all its resources at the disposal of the national committee and becomes its close ally, foregoing its own initiative even in what concerns the congressional elections, for in the "presidential year" all the elections tend to follow the fortunes of the contest for the presidency. "It issues no text book of its own but may assist the national committee in the preparation of such a work" and frequently much of the matter prepared during the four years by the congressional committee is used again in the presidential campaign. "While it may raise funds and aid doubtful districts it must not in the exercise of these functions interfere with the plans of the national campaign committee."[1]

committee in the West had likewise been in charge for some time of the similar bureau for the congressional committee.

[1] J. Macy, *Party Organization and Machinery,* 89.

BIBLIOGRAPHICAL NOTE

SOURCES FOR:

1. *National Conventions.*

    a. Campaign text books published by the national and congressional committees.

    b. Proceedings of the national conventions of the two parties (officialy published and re-published by order of the conventions).

    c. Memoirs of private persons who were present and magazine articles written by such persons.

    d. Contemporary newspaper and magazine accounts as well as contemporary campaign text books, scrap books and hand books of politics.

    e. The convention system is fully treated in Chapters X, XI, XII of J. A. Woodburn's *"Political Parties and Party Problems")*.

    f. An interesting sketch of the history of congressional caucuses and presidential conventions is given by Mr. M. Ostrogorski in two articles in the *Annales de l'Ecole Libre des Sciences Politiques,* January and April, 1888.

    g. The full text of the Republican national platforms from 1856 to 1900 may be found in F. Curtis, *The Republican Party,* I, II, also in T. H. McKee, *National Conventions and Platforms,* and J. Tweedy, *A History of Republican National Conventions.* The platform of any special convention is of course also to be found in the official proceedings of the convention.

    h. The evolution of the present convention is admirably discussed in "The Rise and Fall of the Nominating Caucus, Legislative and Congressional," M. Ostrogorski, *American Historical Review,* Jan., 1900; Vol. V, p. 253.

2. *National Committee.*

    a. The proceedings of the national conventions are the main sources of official information upon the work and organization of the national committee. A discussion of its organization and character is also found in J. Macy, *Party Organization and Machinery.*

b. "This committee receives increasing attention in current literature." "New Powers of the National Committee." R. Ogden, *The Atlantic Monthly,* Vol. LXXXIX, p. 76. "The Republican National Committee; How it works for votes." *Review of Reviews,* Vol. XXII, p. 529. "George B. Cortelyou, and the Republican Campaign," *Review of Reviews,* Vol. XXX, p. 294.. "The Management of the Taft Campaign." *Review of Reviews,* Vol. XXXVIII, p. 432.

c. Direct information from members of the national committee.

3. *State Party Organization.*

a. Direct information from party managers.

b. Printed rules of party committees.

c. Laws regulating the process of nomination; primary election laws.

d. Published proceedings of State party conventions; few and meagre.

e. In some of the States there are outlines of party history with texts of State platforms of the different parties.

f. F. J. Goodnow, "Political Parties and City Government" *Proceedings National Municipal League,* Vol. V (1899).

g. Excellent accounts of party organization in Massachusetts, Indiana and Missouri are contained in J. Macy's *Party Organization and Machinery.*

h. Local party organization especially Republican in New York City, Philadelphia, Baltimore and Boston, is admirably discussed in F. W. Whitridge's *The Caucus System* and F. W. Dallinger's *Nominations for Elective Office in the United States.*

i. C. E. Merriam of Chicago University, "State Central Committees." *Political Science Quarterly,* Vol. XIX, p. 224 (1904). This is a detailed study of the organization of the State party committees in most of the States of the Union.

4. *State Platforms.*

    a. Proceedings of the State conventions. (Sometimes officially published by order of the conventions.)

    b. Campaign text books published by the several State executive or central committees.

    c. All of the State platforms for the year 1871 have been gathered and printed by Hon. Edward McPherson, LLD., Clerk of the House of Representatives in a *Handbook of Politics for 1872* (1872).

5. *Party History, Organization and Machinery Generally.*

    a. "Every new phase in the growth of party machinery has called forth fresh criticism and warning. The literature hostile to the political party is of peculiar importance because of its portrayal of a clear recognition of the party as a distinct political institution." Of these attacks upon the party system, M. Ostrogorski's work, *Democracy and the Organization of Political Parties* is one of the latest and in many respects the most important.

        Those who have written in defense of parties, from a friendly or sympathetic spirit have usually failed to recognize in the American party organization a political institution, extra-legal, unique, peculiar and of the deepest significance. "Party history such as forms a part of campaign literature is not the history of a party, but is rather political history from a partizan standpoint."

    b. Various references to party and faction found in *The Federalist,* illustrate the type of American ideas which prevailed, one might say, before the American party system appeared. (See paper No. X by Madison.)

    c. The following are a few of the many magazine articles which will be found instructive: "The Place of Party in the Political System," Anson D. Morse, *Annals of the American Academy,* Vol. II, No. 3; "The Party Organization," J. Macy, Chicago *Record,* Homestudy Circle, 1900; "Party Government in the United States; The Importance of Government by the Republican Party," George G. Hoar, *The International Monthly,* Oct. 1900. Vol. I.

    d. Official proceedings of the national conventions and party campaign text books.

e. The following general treatises are useful: J. Macy, *Political Parties in the United States;* J. Macy, *Party Organization and Machinery;* J. Bryce, *American Commonwealth;* A. Shaw, *Political Problems of American Development;* C. A. Beard, *American Government and Politics;* J. S. Jenks, *History of Political Parties in New York;* J. H. Hopkins, *History of Political Parties in the United States;* J. A. Woodburn, *Political Parties and Party Problems in the United States;* F. W. Dallinger, *Nominations for Elective Office;* E. C. Meyer, *Nominating Systems;* J. P. Gordy, *History of Political Parties in the United States.* Schouler, Adams, McMaster and Rhodes in their *Histories of the United States* are valuable as well as Stanwood's *History of the Presidency;* McKee's *Party Platforms;* McClure's, *Our Presidents and How We Make Them;* Nicolay and Hay's *Life of Lincoln;* Greeley's *American Conflict;* Benton's *Thirty Years' View;* Blaine's *Twenty Years of Congress;* Burgess' *Middle Period, Civil War and the Constitution, Reconstruction and the Constitution;* Wilson's *Division and Reunion,* and *History of the American People.*

DOCUMENTS AND ORIGINAL SOURCES:

a. Most of the documents referred to in this work are printed at length in the proceedings of the national and State conventions officially published and re-published by order of the conventions, and many of them are also to be found in the collections of pamphlets, and other contemporary records in many of the large libraries in the City of New York.

LIST OF WORKS CONSULTED

Adams, C. F. *Charles Francis Adams* (1900).
Appleton's *Annual Encyclopedia* (1864-83).

Bancroft, F. *Life of William Henry Seward,* I, II (1900).
Beard, C. A. *American Government and Politics* (1910).
Beard, C. A. *Readings in American Government and Politics* (1909).
Benton, T. H. *Thirty Years' View,* I, II (1879).
Bernheim, A. C. *Party Organizations and Their Nominations to Public Office, etc.* Political Science Quarterly, III, 99-123 (1888).
Bigelow, J. *John C. Frémont* (1856).
Bigelow, J. *Samuel J. Tilden's Public Writing and Speeches,* I (1895).
Birney, W. *James G. Birney and His Times* (1890).
Bishop, J. B. *Our Political Drama. Conventions, Campaigns, Candidates* (1904).
Blaine, J. G. *Twenty Years of Congress,* I (1884).
Blanchard, R. *Rise and Fall of Poltical Parties in the United States* (1884).
Boutwell, G. S. *Why I am a Republican* (1884).
Brown, S. G. *Life of Rufus Choate* (1891).
Bryce, J. *The American Commonwealth,* I, II (1906).
Burgess, J. W. *The Civil War and the Constitution* (1903).
Burgess, J. W. *The Middle Period* (1900).
Burgess, J. W. *Political Science and Comparative Constitutional Law,* I, II (1890).
Burk, A. B. *Golden Jubilee of the Republican Party* (1906).

Cambridge Modern History, VII (1903).
Channing, E. & Hart, A. B. *Guide to American History,* §§186, 189, 198, 202 (1896).
Champion, F. *Campaign Hand Book and Manual* (1872).
Cluskey, M. W. *Political Text Book* (1860).
Colton, C. *Works of Henry Clay* (1904).
Congressional Globe, 34th and 35th Congresses (1855-59).
Conkling, A. R. *Life and Letters of Roscoe Conkling* (1889).
Cooley, T. M. *The General Principles of Constitutional Law in the United States of America* (1903).
Cooper, T. V. & Fenton, H. T. *American Politics* (1884).

Curtis, G. T. *Life of Daniel Webster* (1870).
Curtis, F. *The Republican Party,* I, II (1904).

Dallinger, F. W. *Nominations for Elective Office in the United States* (1897).
Detroit *Post and Tribune. Zachariah Chandler* (1880).
Dunning, W. A. *The Second Birth of the Republican Party,* American Historical Review, XVI, 56 (Oct. 1900).

Fiske, J. *Essays, Historical and Literary,* II (1907).
Fiske, J. *Whig Party* (1902).
Flower, F. A. *History of the Republican Party* (1884).
Ford, H. J. *Rise and Growth of American Politics* (1898).

Garrison, W. L. *Westward Extension,* American Nation, XVII, ch. XVI.
Giddings, F. H. *The Principles of Sociology* (1896).
Giddings, J. R. *History of the Rebellion* (1864).
Godkin, E. L. *The Caucus and the Republican Party,* Nation, VII, 4 (1868).
Goodnow, F. J. *Politics and Administration in Government* (1900).
Goodnow, F. J. *American Administrative Law* (1905).
Goodnow, F. J. *Political Parties and City Government;* Proceedings National Municipal League, V (1899).
Goodnow, F. J. *Comparative Administrative Law* (1903).
Gordy, J. P. *History of Political Parties in the United States,* I (1900).
Gordy, J. P. *Political History of the United States,* II (1900).
Greeley, H. *The American Conflict,* I (1864).
Greeley, H. *Political Text Book of 1860* (1860).

Hall, B. F. *The Republican Party and its Candidates* (1856).
Halstead, M. *History of National Political Conventions of the Current Presidential Campaign* (1860).
Hammond, J. D. *History of Political Parties in New York* (1845).
Hart, A. B. *Life of Salmon P. Chase* (1899).
Hoar, G. F. *Autobiography of Seventy Years,* I (1903).
Holmes, A. *Parties and Their Principles* (1859).
Hopkins, J. H. *History of Political Parties in the United States* (1900).
Houghton, W. H. *Conspectus of the History of Political Parties* (1880).

Jenks, J. S. *History of Political Parties in New York* (1894).
Jenks, J. W. *The Fundamental Principles of Politics in the United States from the Viewpoint of the American Citizen* (1909).
Johnston, A. *History of American Politics* (1879).
Johnson, C. W. *Official Proceedings of Republican National Conventions* (1856, 1860, 1864, 1868, 1872, 1876, 1880, 1884, 1888, 1892, 1896, 1900, 1904).
Julian, G. W. *Political Recollections* (1884).
Julian, G. W. *The First Republican National Convention*, American Historical Review, IV, 313 (1899).

Lalor, J. J. *Cyclopaedia of Political Science*, II, III (1893).
Landon, J. S. *Constitutional History and Government of the United States* (1904).
Lawton, G. W. *The American Caucus System* (1885).
Lodge, H. C. *Daniel Webster* (1893).
Long, J. D. *The Republican Party* (1888).
Lothrop, T. J. *William Henry Seward* (1896).

McClure, A. K. *Recollections of Half a Century* (1902).
McClure, A. K. *Our Presidents and How We Make Them* (1902).
McClure, A. K. *Abraham Lincoln and Men of War Times* (1892).
McCulloch, H. *Men and Measures of Half a Century* (1888).
McKee, T. H. *National Conventions and Platforms* (1900).
McLaughlin, A. C. *Lewis Cass* (1899).
McMaster, J. B. *Life of Thurlow Weed* (1896).
McPherson, E. *Political History of the United States during the Great Rebellion* (1876).
McPherson, E. *Handbooks of Politics for 1868, 1872 and 1876.*
MacDonald, W. *Select Documents Illustrative of the History of the United States* (1898).
Macy, J. *Party Organization and Machinery* (1904).
Macy, J. *Political Parties in the United States*, 1846-1861 (1900).
Macy, J. *History of Political Parties in the United States* (1897).
Maverick, A. *Raymond and New York Journalism* (1870).
Mead, E. D., ed. *South Carolina Leaflets.*
Merriam, C. E. *Primary Elections* (1908).
Meyer, E. C. *Nomination Methods* (1902).
Morgan, J. T. *Party Conventions.* North American Review, CLV, 237 (1892).
Morse, I. T. *Abraham Lincoln.*
Münsterberg, H. *The Americans* (1904).

Nation (1865-83).

New York *Times* (1854-64).
New York *Tribune.* Daily and Weekly (1854-64).
Nicolay, J. G. and Hay, J. *Abraham Lincoln,* I, II, IX (1905).
Niles' *Weekly Register,* LXX (1846).

Official Proceedings of the First Three Republican National Conventions of 1856, 1860 and 1864, prepared and published under the direction of the Republican national convention of 1892.[1] Also the official proceedings for 1868, 1872, 1876, 1880, 1884, 1888,[2] 1892, 1896, 1900, 1904 and 1908.

Ormsby, R. McK. *History of the Whig Party* (1860).
Ostrogorski, M. *Democracy and the Organization of Political Parties,* I, II (1902).

Patton, J. H. *Democratic Party, Its Political History and Influence* (1884).
Pierce, E. L. *Charles Sumner* (1893).
Pike, J. S. *First Blows of the Civil War* (1879).
Polk, J. K. *The Diary of J. K. Polk during his Presidency, 1845-1849* (1910).
Putnam, J. O. *Addresses. Principles of he Republican Party* (1886).
Raymond, H. J. *Life, Public Services and State Papers of Abraham Lincoln* (1865).
Remsen, D. S. *Primary Elections* (1900).
Rhodes, J. F. *History of the United States from the Compromise of 1850,* I, II, III (1901).
Roosevelt, T. *Thomas H. Benton* (1887).
Roosevelt, T. *American Ideals* (1897).

[1] The secretary of the Republican national convention of 1892 at Minneapolis, was directed to prepare and have published the proceedings of the first three Republican conventions, viz.: of the years 1856 at Philadelphia, 1860 at Chicago, and 1864 at Baltimore. The volume also includes proceedings of the antecedent national Republican convention held at Pittsburg in February, 1856, as reported by Horace Greeley, a most valuable reprint and a sketch of the earliest Republican national organization on record.

[2] The official proceedings from 1868-1888 have all been reprinted under the direction of the national committee, by authority of a resolution of the Republican national convention of 1900.

These official reprints are uniformly cited in the text.

Schouler, J. *History of the United States* (1894-1904).

Schucker, J. W. *Life of Salmon P. Chase* (1874).

Schurz, C. *Henry Clay* (1899).

Schurz, C. *Reminiscences of Carl Schurz* (1907).

Seilhaimer, G. O. *Leslie's History of the Republican Party*, I (1900).

Seward, W. H. *Works of W. H. Seward,* IV (1853-90).

Shaler, N. S. *The Citizen* (1904).

Shaw, A. *Political Problems of Ameican Development* (1907).

Shepard, E. M. *Martin Van Buren* (1888).

Sherman, J. *Recollections of Forty Years* (1895).

Smalley, E. V. *The Republican Party* (1880).

Smith, H. H. *All the Republican National Conventions* (1892).

Smith, G. *Political History of the United States* (1892).

Smith, T. C. *The Liberty and Free-Soil Parties in the Northwest* (1897).

Smith, T. C. *Parties and Slavery* (1850-1859). (American Nation, Vol. XVIII, edited by A. B. Hart.) (1905.)

Stanwood, E. *History of the Presidency* (1898).

Stanwood, E. *American Tariff Controversies in the Nineteenth Century,* II (1903).

Stephens, A. H. *War between the States,* II (1868).

Storey, M. *Life of Charles Sumner* (1900).

Sumner, W. G. *Politics in America, 1876* (1876).

Sumner, C. *Speech on the Republican Party* (1860).

Thompson, D. G. *Politics in Democracy* (1890).

Thorpe, F. N. *Constitutional History of the United States,* I, II, III (1901).

Tribune *Almanac. Annual Volumes* (1855-61).

Tucker, J. R. *The Constitution of the United States, a Critical Discussion of its Genesis, etc.* (1899).

Turner, A. J. *Genesis of the Republican Party* (1891).

Tweedy, J. *History of the Republican National Conventions from 1856 to 1898* (1910).

Van Buren, M. *Origin of Political Parties in the United States* (1827).

Von Holst, H. E. *Constitutional and Political History of the United States,* IV, V, VI (1877-1892).

Weed, T. *Autobiography of Thurlow Weed,* I, II (1884).

Whig *Almanac. Annual Volumes* (1851-1855).

Whitridge, F. W. *Caucus System* (1883).

Willey, A. *History of the Anti-Slavery Cause in the State and Nation* (1886).

Wilson, H. *History of the Rise and Fall of the Slave Power in America,* II (1872).

Wilson, W. *Division and Reunion* (1893).

Wilson, W. *Constitutional Government in the United States* (1908).

Wilson, W. *The State* (1901).

Winsor, J. *Narrative and Critical History of America,* VII (1888).

Woodburn, J. A. *Political Parties and Problems in the United States* (1903).

Also the collections of numerous pamphlets, Republican campaign text books, scrap books and handbooks of politics, addresses of local Republican clubs and of State and City central committees and other contemporary political tracts and contemporary records of State and local conventions and mass meetings and of the national conventions in the Columbia, Astor, Lenox and Mercantile Libraries in the City of New York.

VITA

The author was born in 1883 at the City of New York and received his preparatory education in Sachs' Collegiate Institute. In 1901 he entered Columbia College, and devoted his attention principally to the study of History and Political Science.

In 1904 he began the study of Law in the Law School of Columbia University and in 1905 received his Bachelor of Arts degree; continuing his study of Political Science and History under Professors Burgess, Goodnow and Moore until 1906, when the degree of Master of Arts was conferred upon him. The author remained in residence at the Law School, receiving in 1907 a Bachelor of Laws degree, and then obtained a year's leave of absence, returning in June, 1908, to have the degree of Master of Laws conferred upon him.

In 1907 he passed the oral examinations for the degree of Doctor of Philosophy.